PROFITABLE
PODCASTING

PROFITABLE
PODCASTING

GROW YOUR BUSINESS, EXPAND YOUR PLATFORM, AND

BUILD A NATION OF TRUE FANS

STEPHEN WOESSNER

◆AMACOM

AMERICAN MANAGEMENT ASSOCIATION
New York • Atlanta • Brussels • Chicago • Mexico City • San Francisco
Shanghai • Tokyo • Toronto • Washington, DC

Bulk discounts available. For details visit:
www.amacombooks.org/go/specialsales
Or contact special sales:
Phone: 800-250-5308
E-mail: specialsls@amanet.org
View all the AMACOM titles at: www.amacombooks.org
American Management Association: www.amanet.org

This publication is designed to provide accurate and authoritative information in regard to the subject matter covered. It is sold with the understanding that the publisher is not engaged in rendering legal, accounting, or other professional service. If legal advice or other expert assistance is required, the services of a competent professional person should be sought.

Library of Congress Cataloging-in-Publication Data

Names: Woessner, Stephen, 1972- author.
Title: Profitable podcasting : grow your business, expand your platform, and
    build a nation of true fans / Stephen Woessner.
Description: New York : Amacom, [2017] | Includes bibliographical references
    and index.
Identifiers: LCCN 2017010664 (print) | LCCN 2017013242 (ebook) | ISBN
    9780814438299 (E-book) | ISBN 9780814438282 (pbk.)
Subjects: LCSH: Internet marketing. | Podcasting.
Classification: LCC HF5415.1265 (ebook) | LCC HF5415.1265 .W64 2017 (print) |
    DDC 658.8/72—dc23
LC record available at https://lccn.loc.gov/2017010664

About AMA

American Management Association (www.amanet.org) is a world leader in talent development, advancing the skills of individuals to drive business success. Our mission is to support the goals of individuals and organizations through a complete range of products and services, including classroom and virtual seminars, webcasts, webinars, podcasts, conferences, corporate and government solutions, business books, and research. AMA's approach to improving performance combines experiential learning—learning through doing—with opportunities for ongoing professional growth at every step of one's career journey.

10 9 8 7 6 5 4 3 2 1

CONTENTS

CONTENTS

ACKNOWLEDGMENTS

To Christine and Caitlyn—I appreciate your love and support in every challenge I tackle. You make me want to strive to be a better husband, father, and person. I love you to the moon and back—and always will.

To my grandfather, Peter Maronitis—you spent your life in service of others. It was you who taught me the value of mentorship, hard work, and commitment to family. You lived a life worthy of following. I look forward to our conversations again. I love you, Pop.

To Don Yaeger and Drew McLellan—thank you for being great friends and trusted mentors. You know how to get the best out of me. I appreciate you more than you will ever know.

To Wendy Keller—this book would not have been possible without you. You planted the seed and then you gave me the road map to follow. Thank you so much for being my wonderful agent, mentor, and friend.

To our Predictive ROI clients and our *Onward Nation* guests—you have helped my team and me grow in new ways, you pushed us to be better, and you generously shared your expertise with our listeners—and with me directly—so we could all move onward to that next level. Thank you so very much, my friends!

To Ellen Kadin and the team at AMACOM—thank you for this opportunity, and I greatly appreciate all your support, encouragement, and pushing to make sure the ideas and thoughts in our book were the best possible. Exceptional teamwork! Thank you! Thank you!

Thank you for picking up our book. Congratulations on taking the first step toward growing your revenue, expanding your platform, and building your nation of true fans. Herein lies everything you need to make your vision a reality. Time to get to work!

FOREWORD

Why are some teams capable of being great and sustaining their high performance over a long period of time—while others can't? We see it happen not just in sports. We also see it happen in business teams with companies like Starbucks, Southwest Airlines, members of the *Inc.* 500 list, and so on.

How are they able to consistently outperform their competition time and time again?

I have studied the best-of-the-best team builders in sports and in business over the last twenty-five years and uncovered what makes the great teams great. I have witnessed how great teams are in constant study of other great teams to learn what they need to come together, to manage adversity as a group, to find a common purpose, to protect their inner circle, and more.

If you believe as I do that success leaves clues—then our job as business leaders is to go find the clues and apply them within our teams. But . . . are we as leaders willing to invest the time and energy to study what it takes to move our businesses onward to that next level?

In my opinion, one of the best ways to learn from the experiences of others, and to uncover the clues to their success, is to invite them to participate in a platform like a YouTube channel, blog, or a top-rated podcast so you can interview them and allow them to share their knowledge and expertise with your audience. By doing so, you will learn directly from the experts—and—you will expand your inner circle in the process. Your personal network and your sphere of influence will grow, and it is likely that new business development opportunities will find their way to you.

You are holding in your hands a precise blueprint to make the above a reality. *Profitable Podcasting* does not include marketing hyperbole. You must be willing to do the work. Stephen Woessner and his Predictive ROI team have shared in full transparency all the practical knowledge you need to create, launch, and monetize a top-rated podcast that can accelerate your business. The success clues have been distilled into specific strategies and step-by-step instructions that you and your team can immediately apply.

You will learn how your podcast can become an "all access pass" to the knowledge of others if you are courageous enough to knock on the doors and ask the questions. Stephen will also teach you how your podcast can become a distinctive business development strategy to grow your revenue. He calls it the "Trojan Horse of Sales," and I have seen him do it for Predictive ROI and repeat the same success for its clients.

I am a firm believer that greatness is available to all of us if we are willing to do the common things uncommonly well. But, there is no such thing as an overnight success. So I also want to share some behind-the-scenes context with you.

In addition to being close friends, Stephen and I are weekly accountability partners; we talk every Friday morning and share our wins and losses for the week and how we expect to get better as a result of what we learned. We have rinsed and repeated this weekly process since August of 2012. I remember our Friday call back in May 2015 when he shared his inspiration behind *Onward Nation* and what he and his team had decided to do. He explained their goal to launch a daily show for business owners. I thought their plan was ambitious but was excited to hear the enthusiasm in Stephen's voice. I know what can happen when business owners are intentional about surrounding themselves with winners.

As an award-winning keynote speaker, business leadership coach, and longtime associate editor for *Sports Illustrated*, I have experienced firsthand how spending time with thought leaders and learning from the best can dramatically impact the trajectory of one's business and life. I knew Stephen would be successful if he and his team could be consistent with their strategy and had the discipline to remain consistent in their pursuit of greatness.

The results are now clear.

Onward Nation has generated over $2 million in revenue for Predictive ROI—and—I have watched Stephen's personal network expand to include some of today's top business owners, thought leaders, and authors. *Onward Nation* is now listened to in more than one hundred countries, it has received exceptional ratings and reviews, and there is a three-month waiting list to appear as a guest.

There are no secrets to being successful at podcasting and using it as a business development strategy to move onward to that next level. It is all here for you in this book. You simply need to be willing to do the common things uncommonly well.

As Coach John Wooden said, "Make each day your masterpiece."

—DON YAEGER
Nine-time *New York Times* bestselling author

PROFITABLE
PODCASTING

HOW A PODCAST CAN BE YOUR TROJAN HORSE OF SELLING

We learn by doing. So, if you desire to master the principles you are studying in this book, do something about them. Apply these rules at every opportunity. If you don't you will forget them quickly. Only knowledge that is used sticks in your mind.

—DALE CARNEGIE, *How to Win Friends and Influence People*

My name is Stephen Woessner. I am the CEO of Predictive ROI (a content marketing and lead agency) and the host of *Onward Nation*, a daily podcast for business owners. Our mission at *Onward Nation* is to be America's number one podcast for learning how today's top business owners think, act, and achieve. We immediately struck a powerful chord with listeners: *Onward Nation* became a top-ranked podcast within iTunes' New and Noteworthy in multiple categories just three weeks after airing Episode 1 with author Scott McKain on June 15, 2015.

Onward Nation is now listened to in more than 200 countries, has received 100,000+ downloads of its episodes, and will generate *$2 million in revenue for Predictive ROI over the next twelve months.*

But how did we do all of that? We learned *Onward Nation* could become our Trojan horse.

Your Trojan Horse of Selling

The legend of the Trojan horse comes from the story of the Trojan War between the Greeks and Troy chronicled in the *Odyssey*, written by Homer near the end of the 8th century BC. The story—which could be fact or fiction—is a great illustration of strategy and subterfuge.

According to the legend, the Trojan War ended in a stalemate because Greece was unable to devise a strategy to circumvent the city walls of Troy. The ten-year battle ended and the Greek army made what looked to be a retreat to their homeland.

The Trojan army investigated and found the beach abandoned. The Greek armada was gone and a large wooden horse was all that remained on the desolate shore. The Trojans believed the Greeks had left the horse as a peace offering. They gleefully accepted the offering and pulled the horse from the beach, past their impenetrable city gates, into the city square, and began to celebrate their victory over the Greeks.

However, a little due diligence by the Trojans would have been prudent. Perhaps they would have found the Greek strike force tucked inside the horse. The Greeks seized their opportunity late that night when they sneaked quietly out of the horse and opened the city gates so the balance of their army could enter unencumbered.

The Greeks proceeded to sack the city. The story gave birth to the expression "Beware a Greek bearing gifts."

The monetization strategy behind your podcast, if executed properly, will work in a similar way. For example, a typical salesperson may have access to a decision-maker within a dream prospect's company blocked by a "gatekeeper." Any sort of sales opportunity is thwarted, and the salesperson may be forced to move on to her next prospect.

However, what if you happen to be the host of a top-rated podcast and you are getting in touch with the decision-maker because you would like to interview him about his journey, his secrets to success, and the wisdom he could share with others in his industry or the broader business community? Well, now, you just changed the entire dynamic of the situation, didn't you? Your podcast increased the probability of a one-on-one, private, sixty-minute conversation with your ideal prospect.

But how did your podcast give you this "all-access pass"? Your podcast changed the game because you are no longer perceived as a business owner looking for a new account. You are now perceived as a *journalist* and your show is a *media channel*—a conduit—to an audience the guests on your show want to reach and influence.

It's as simple as letting the decision-maker at your dream prospect wheel the horse past the company's gatekeeper—and park it right in the center of the C-suite. You now have an opportunity to dazzle your dream prospect with your brilliance and intimate industry and company knowledge during the interview.

Your podcast has done its job. It's time for you to do yours. Sell!

Our Story and Why You Need This Book

It was a quiet Sunday afternoon in the middle of May 2015. I was sitting at my dining room table looking out the front window at my daughter and her friends having fun at our neighborhood playground. All was well outside—but not inside. I was under a great deal of stress.

We had just lost a client. And although every company experiences this from time to time, what made this particular loss so painful was that we were over-staffed. The loss in revenue made our reality even more excruciating.

I had purchased the domain name OnwardNation.com about twelve months earlier but had no idea why. No strategy; I just felt compelled to make the purchase. Funny how God whispers the seeds of inspiration into your ear sometimes and then just lets them sit until He is ready for them to germinate into something remarkable.

That Sunday must have been germination day. As I sat there at my dining room table, I remembered the OnwardNation.com purchase and made the decision that we would create and launch a daily podcast using that name. Next,

I crafted an enthusiastic, optimistic email explaining that *Onward Nation* was the solution we'd been seeking to turn Predictive ROI lead generation and sales activity around (mind you, I had zero strategy, only unbridled optimism). In the email I set an aggressive launch date of June 15. I closed the lid to my MacBook, and somehow felt good about the decision (or chaos) that I had just initiated.

Why chaos, you ask? Well, I should probably share that the decision to create and launch a podcast in thirty days was made in complete and utter ignorance. I knew nothing about creating or launching a podcast.

Sure, I had been a guest on a couple of podcasts such as *EOFire* with John Lee Dumas and *ReLaunch* with Joel Boggess and Dr. Pei Kang. So I knew how to put on a headset and open Skype, which constituted my entire body of knowledge in the podcast world up to that point.

Let's fast-forward to launch day, Monday, June 15. Remarkably, we launched on schedule and the first day of *Onward Nation* ran smoothly. We aired three episodes on launch day: Episode 1 with Scott McKain, Episode 2 with sports journalist and author Don Yaeger, and Episode 3 with leadership coach Stacey Alcorn. All three guests are rock stars, and *Onward Nation* was off and running.

Several weeks later, I attended my Agency Management Institute mastermind group. By then, *Onward Nation* had aired forty-seven episodes, daily downloads were steadily increasing, and we had scored top rankings in iTunes. I was feeling proud about our accomplishments. We had gone from zero to sixty in about 3.5 seconds. Not bad. But we were missing a vital outcome: revenue!

My mastermind group—all exceptional agency owners from across the country—asked me how I was going to make money from *Onward Nation*. Excellent question, but I had no idea of the answer. "I don't know," I said. "But we will figure it out."

Then providence set in. Two of our *Onward Nation* guests got in touch with me and asked, "Hey, could you do that for me?"

"Do what for you?" I asked.

"Build me a podcast!" they said.

Like any enthusiastic entrepreneur in need of revenue, I said, "Yes, I think we can!"

So my team and I stripped out the branding and content from the *Onward Nation* system and replaced everything with our client's branding, episodes, content—and voila! We launched two more podcasts and earned $26,000 for our effort. Rock-solid awesome!

Now, a smart businessperson would have said, "Hey, we might be onto something here. This could be worth pursuing." But I didn't say that. Instead, I returned to thinking about how we were overstaffed and needed to grow revenue. Ironic, isn't it? I often say that if God wants me to get the message, He needs to take out a billboard or hit me over the head with a brick. Subtlety is lost on me.

In late October, one of those clients (Drew McLellan, host of the *Build a Better Agency* podcast) said to me, "The podcast you built for me is awesome. And *Onward Nation* is awesome. Why in the world are you not building more of these?" In my brilliance, I said, "For who?" Drew rolled his eyes and said, "There have to be more *Onward Nation* guests who would love to have a podcast of their own!"

He took the lesson he was teaching me deeper, adding, "Look, here's what you do. You create a Silver, Gold, and Platinum Elite package . . . you charge this much, this much, and this much, and get out there and sell them to guests."

Brilliant. My team and I immediately got to work creating the packages Drew had recommended.

And then providence struck a second time. On November 17, 2015, I interviewed Wendy Keller, literary agent extraordinaire, for Episode 106 of *Onward Nation*. The conversation started out lovely—just what I had envisioned. Then, suddenly, I felt like I'd been punched in the stomach and the air knocked right out of me. Wendy told her emotional and devastating story about the tragic car accident that she and her husband, along with their two children, were in while on vacation in Europe. Her children were killed, she was critically injured, and her life was changed in an instant. My legs felt weak. In shock, I didn't know what to say. Wendy had to be the strongest person I'd ever met. After continuing for a few minutes, she paused and gave me a moment to catch my breath. Then we continued the interview. I was captivated by Wendy's courage, her commitment, and her resolve. What could stop this woman?

When we finished the interview, she turned the tables on me, asking about *Onward Nation*. Why was I doing it? What was the endgame? I told her I was planning to write a book that distilled all the wisdom collected during the episodes of the podcast. I could practically feel her smile on the other end of our Skype connection. And then she asked me a life-altering question: "Hmm … Why don't you write a book about how business owners can use podcasting to grow revenue and their business? That's where the real opportunity is for a book." Bam. Providence!

Following the interview with Wendy, my Predictive ROI team made it a vital priority to accelerate the sales of our newly minted Silver, Gold, and Platinum Elite packages. We were on a mission to create a bona fide monetization strategy. Our goal was to grow revenue, and at the same time, create a compelling proof of concept for the system that would eventually become this book.

We grew podcast-related revenue to $223,000 between November 17 and December 31, 2015, and built a sales pipeline of $380,000 during Q1 2016. We scaled our production and sales teams and created step-by-step documentation of our system. Currently, we predict *$2 million in podcast-related revenue during the next twelve months.*

We accomplished this thanks in part to several amazing mentors who stepped into our path. We listened to them, and we did exactly what they recommended. We are now building a network of B2B-focused podcasts—the "Onward Nation Network." By the end of 2017, we expect Predictive ROI to be the company behind approximately a hundred top-ranked business podcasts with millions of listeners worldwide.

It has been an amazing adventure. But your story of growing your business, expanding your platform, and building a nation of true fans can be just as amazing. This book will serve as your comprehensive guide to making your dream a reality—and in the process you will learn how to avoid all of the mistakes we made along the way.

This comprehensive, research-based book will share our full blueprint or "recipe" for podcast success with you. Each and every step we took along the way is presented in complete transparency. Not a single step has been hidden from you. It's all here, in plain sight.

Within these pages, you will walk behind the green curtains of *Onward Nation* and Predictive ROI so you can learn our proven system. You will also have access to in-depth insights from ten business owners just like you. Each of them decided to create a podcast to change the game—and then did it. Their impressive stories will be shared in full transparency, too.

But why write such a comprehensive book? Because you deserve a resource that eliminates the guesswork, demystifies the process, and gives you a clear and concise strategy for going *from zero to launch in about thirty days.*

Only limited resources were available when my Predictive ROI team and I decided to create *Onward Nation*. Sure, there were plenty of e-books and webinars that led me into the sales funnels of information marketers, but those resources lacked depth, and, candidly, they lacked business acumen. We quickly consumed the resources and were left with more questions than answers.

Plus, the resources lacked full transparency. They typically provided just enough to get you interested in learning more and then pitched a $997 online training or mastermind program.

All of which drove me crazy and didn't solve our problem. Not awesome.

But there is another reason I decided to go as deep as possible with this book. In my opinion, podcasting—as a medium—deserves a long-form guide, an encyclopedia of how to do it right. When I interviewed Gary Vaynerchuk before the release of his social media book *Jab, Jab, Jab, Right Hook*, we discussed how it wasn't just a social media book, but a business book that would elevate social media to a new level of legitimacy.[1]

My hope is that this book will raise the bar for podcasting just as Gary did for social media marketing. On the surface, *Profitable Podcasting* looks like a podcasting book. But it's actually a business book about how business owners are using podcasting to grow their companies, expand their platforms, and build nations of true fans. Each chapter includes step-by-step instructions so you can create, launch, market, and monetize your own podcast. The book includes checklists, production schedules, weekly goal tracking, social media strategies with visual examples, promotional emails, guest invitations, exclusive access to private online video tutorials, and other resources including time-saving third-party tools.

I am excited to share this resource because small business has been my focus for twenty-three years. This is my third book devoted to helping small-business owners succeed.

Helping small-business owners is deeply rewarding for several reasons. First, having owned five small businesses, I know that in today's economy if one wants to have an impact (as I strive to do), then small business represents a tremendous opportunity. Small-business owners are the lifeblood of our economy.

Second, the 28 million small businesses operating in the United States today, according to the Small Business Administration, account for 55 percent of all jobs and 54 percent of total revenue generated.[2] I want to help as many business owners as possible grow so they can create more jobs and improve the lives of their families, employees, and communities.

Third, this book tackles the top challenge facing most business owners: According to a recent survey of 1,100 small business owners, 43 percent of respondents identified *growing revenue as a top challenge facing U.S. businesses in 2016.*[3] That's more than *12 million businesses expected to face the same challenge.*[4]

Driving this number down is a worthy goal of this book.

Podcasting Is Still in Rapid-Growth Mode

Before we dive into the system, I want to take a moment to share some important data points to give you the confidence to move forward and launch your own podcast. I don't want you to fall into the tempting mental trap of thinking that you "waited too long to get started" and, because of that time lost, you somehow "missed your window of opportunity." Cast low-quality thoughts like this aside.

Rest assured, you have not missed the podcasting wave. The sun has not set on your opportunity. *This is the perfect time for you to get started.*

In fact, this may be the perfect time to get started because the trailblazers have gone before you. A path has been marked, and you can learn from their successes and failures. Your learning curve will be shorter so that growing your business, expanding your platform, and building your nation of true fans will be the most efficient it has been for any business owner up to this point.

Sounds awesome, doesn't it?

Podcasting, despite all of its recent growth, is still in its infancy. Getting started now means you still have the opportunity to ride the momentum of what is now a proven medium—and you can use that momentum for your benefit.

Here are some highlights from independent, third-party research that reinforces the importance of getting started now. Thank you to Tom Webster and the team at Edison Research and Triton for generously providing the research.

Figure I-1 illustrates the steady increase in monthly podcast listening. Interestingly, for the five-year period from 2009 through 2013, around 12 percent of the total U.S. population age 12 and over listened to podcasts. In 2016, that number increased to 21 percent, which represents a 75 percent jump in just three years. Impressive.

FIGURE I-1

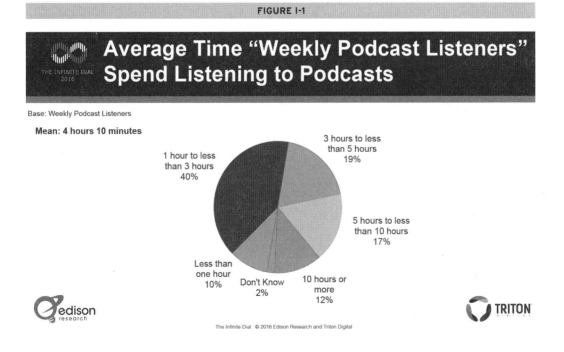

Average Time "Weekly Podcast Listeners" Spend Listening to Podcasts

Base: Weekly Podcast Listeners

Mean: 4 hours 10 minutes

1 hour to less than 3 hours 40%

3 hours to less than 5 hours 19%

5 hours to less than 10 hours 17%

10 hours or more 12%

Don't Know 2%

Less than one hour 10%

The Infinite Dial © 2016 Edison Research and Triton Digital

Bottom line: Monthly podcast listening continues to grow and is trending higher as the ease of listening to podcasts on mobile devices continues to improve.

Edison and Triton also worked to quantify annual household income of podcast listeners as compared to the household income of the total U.S. population age 18 and over. In Figure I-2, we can see that median annual household income in the U.S. population is $53,000. However, the median annual household income of podcast consumers—within the same age range—is $63,000, which represents an increase of 18.86 percent. But even more striking, 41 percent of podcast listeners earn annual household incomes of $75,000 or more, with 15 percent of listeners earning $150,000 or more, versus 9 percent for non-podcast consumers.

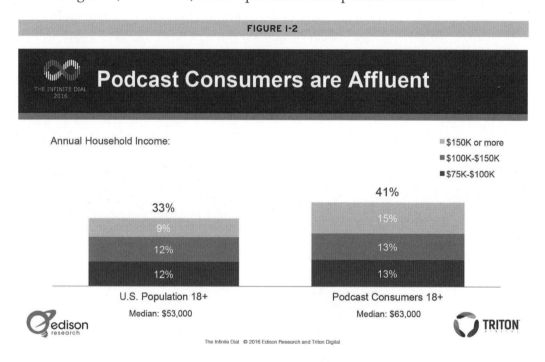

FIGURE I-2

Podcast Consumers are Affluent

THE INFINITE DIAL 2016

Annual Household Income:

■ $150K or more
■ $100K-$150K
■ $75K-$100K

U.S. Population 18+ — 33% (9%, 12%, 12%) — Median: $53,000

Podcast Consumers 18+ — 41% (15%, 13%, 13%) — Median: $63,000

edison research — TRITON

The Infinite Dial © 2016 Edison Research and Triton Digital

Bottom line: Podcast consumers are affluent and likely have disposable income to spend on your products and services.

The percentage of the U.S. population listening to podcasts and the affluence of that audience are compelling points, but how much time do consumers actually spend listening to podcasts? In Figure I-3 we can see that 12 percent of podcast listeners spend ten hours or more per week, with the majority spending

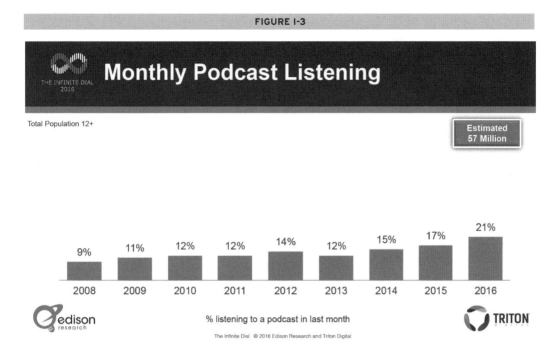

FIGURE I-3

Monthly Podcast Listening

THE INFINITE DIAL 2016

Total Population 12+

Estimated 57 Million

9% — 2008
11% — 2009
12% — 2010
12% — 2011
14% — 2012
12% — 2013
15% — 2014
17% — 2015
21% — 2016

edison research

% listening to a podcast in last month

TRITON

The Infinite Dial © 2016 Edison Research and Triton Digital

one to three hours per week. That is a lot of listening and likely speaks to the increasing popularity of on-demand content based on the specific topics we as consumers want to learn more about.

We will likely see more shows going even more niche to cater to smaller audiences who are extremely passionate about the content being delivered. *This is your opportunity to create your nation of true fans.*

Bottom line: If you aired one high-quality podcast episode per week, and your episode was thirty to forty-five minutes long, the majority of your listeners could easily fit that into their schedule.

You can review the full report from Edison Research at: http://www.edison-research.com/media-research/podcast-research/.

Why Write This Book?

I mentioned earlier that helping small-business owners succeed is deeply rewarding to me for several reasons. But it gets more personal than that. I was raised in my family's restaurants, where I learned entrepreneurial lessons that I still rely on today. I had the privilege and honor to work alongside my mother, aunts, uncles, and cousins while growing up. My grandfather, Peter Maronitis, gave us that gift.

He grew up in Istanbul, Turkey, and was forced to drop out of the third grade to take care of his mother and two younger siblings when his father was tragically killed. That one devastating event changed the future of my entire family. He became the man of the house and had to earn an income so the family could survive. He succeeded, and through the adversity, sparked a dream to make his way to America.

He got his chance when he was 18 years old. With ten dollars in his pocket he arrived in New York City and then eventually settled in Canton, Ohio, where a large Greek community was already flourishing.

He found work in a restaurant where he would clean dishes and cut lettuce on the night shift. After just six years, he had managed to save enough money to open The Ideal Restaurant in downtown Canton.

The year was 1926—just three years before The Great Depression. Not a wise time to open a business. But his business plan was simple, "*If you take care of your customers, they will take care of you. Everyone has to eat.*" He met his future wife, Julia, they got married, ran the restaurant through the Depression, and had four amazing kids along the way. They built a life based on hard work, grit, persistence, tenacity, and a commitment to family.

My grandfather taught us how to be good people by sharing all we have with anyone who needs it. This book represents an opportunity for me to help the millions of small-business owners by sharing how to overcome the challenge of growing revenue. This book is—in some small way—part of his legacy.

I want to say thank you for picking up a copy of this book. It is an honor. I am delighted you chose this book to be what you study and implement into your business.

Onward with gusto!

—*Stephen Woessner*

CHAPTER 1

OVERCOME YOUR BIGGEST OBSTACLES TO SUCCESS

On the surface, this book looks a lot like a book about podcasting—which it is. But it's more than that. My team and I worked tirelessly to make this the deepest, most comprehensive resource we could assemble on the topic of podcasting for small-business owners trying to grow their businesses. I promise you will find that every aspect of creating, producing, launching, and promoting your podcast to grow your business is covered in precise detail within these pages.

Each of the technical systems are dissected, including every piece of software, the specific content in template form you will need for the systems, the guest advocacy process, how to set up distribution channels, site traffic, and analytics and why they matter, along with what it all means. We've even included success stories from a number of small-business owners who are using podcasting as a strategy to grow revenue and build true fans. Each story examines the business model and specifically how podcasting is adding value so you can apply the same principles to your business.

Nothing has been left out. It's all here.

But there is more—much more—that a small-business owner needs to know about podcasting before jumping into the deep end of the pool.

A podcast is just a tool. It's just a platform. A platform is simply a conduit for distributing or sharing content. No platform in and of itself will help your business grow revenue.

Therefore, in order for your podcast to be of value to your business, there needs to be purpose behind the guests you invite to be on your show. There needs to be purpose behind the questions you ask your guests. There needs to be purpose behind how you nurture and take care of your guests before their interviews and after their episodes have aired. Ultimately, you need a strategy for how your podcast will grow your business, expand your platform, and build your nation of true fans.

Having interviewed nearly 600 of today's top business owners—and having talked with, consulted with, or worked with many of them in producing and launching their own podcasts—I can say with certainty that there are typically three primary challenges that arise in the mind of a business owner who is considering podcasting. Some business owners need to confront all three, others perhaps just two. But every business owner will need to confront at least one.

1. How will my podcast make money and help grow my business?
2. How much time will this take me?
3. How will I get guests? (Or, the variation: What if no one accepts my invitation to be a guest on the show?)

We will address the revenue question throughout the book. But, we will dive deep into questions 2 and 3 right now because they are critically important to getting your mindset right before heading down the podcasting path. If you don't get your mindset right, I assure you, there will be setbacks and challenges along the way. Without the correct preparation you will be tempted to quit—and you likely will. However, if I help you properly set expectations, when the challenges come your way, instead of being tempted to quit, you can confidently say to yourself, "Ah, Stephen said this would happen and that I'd feel this way," and you will push forward.

Don't ever quit.

Avoid the Time Trap

One of the questions I am asked most often by business owners who have considered a podcast for their business is, "How much time will having a podcast take out of my schedule?" It's a great question because we should all protect our schedules.

Most business owners assume the answer is ten hours a week—and that the solution will require them to add staff and make other investments. But here's the reality: You can have an awesome, top-rated podcast in iTunes by investing *less than four hours per month*. Yes. Four hours. The system described in this book illustrates our entire process and shows how to duplicate the strategy and the results in as little as four hours per month.

Would you grow revenues faster if you invested more time? Likely yes, but four hours a month is an excellent place to start.

So why would business owners assume that my answer would be ten hours a week? Because then it would be easy for them to justify why they hadn't pursued it more seriously. But in fact, it isn't the perceived time commitment that stops a small-business owner from having a podcast.

It is *fear*.

Fear often rears its ugly head in an attempt to derail the entrepreneurial journey you're on. Fear will beat you to your knees if you let it. Fear will cheat you out of success in all aspects of your business, including developing a great platform like a podcast so you can grow revenue and build a nation of true fans.

Once business owners are assured that their time investment will be only about four hours per month, a second challenge typically comes to mind—one with the subconscious goal of thwarting the podcast from gaining any additional momentum, to snuff out the fire that was building.

Your Biggest, Most Painful Challenge

"Stephen, how will I get guests?" Or the variation: "What if no one accepts the invitation to be on my show?" These two fear-laden questions should serve as warning signs that something sinister is lurking. If you let them, they will keep you in check and prevent you from moving forward. The truth is, we all face such challenges. It's just that some people are better than others at pushing themselves past them.

In my opinion, this challenge may be blocking your success not just with podcasting, but in other areas of your business as well.

The challenge is known as the "impostor syndrome."

Clinical psychologists Pauline R. Clance and Suzanne Imes coined the term in 1978 to describe high-achieving individuals who are unable to internalize their accomplishments and who consequently fear being exposed as a "fraud." Actual, objective evidence of their competence doesn't matter to those who exhibit the syndrome. They remain convinced that they're frauds. They feel that they don't deserve the success they have achieved. Calling it "luck" or "good timing," they never take credit for their accomplishments. Perhaps they believe that they've tricked others into thinking they are more intelligent and competent than they actually are.

Now let's take that definition and break it down into its two core ingredients.

Ingredient #1: the inability to internalize accomplishments and a persistent fear of being exposed as a "fraud."

Have you ever walked into a meeting and felt that you weren't worthy— or that you didn't belong there? Perhaps someone on the selection committee, award committee, or board of directors had made a mistake in selecting you. Heck, maybe even some of your colleagues, family members, or friends validated your own suspicions and asked you the seemingly innocent question, "So why did they pick you?"

I began to learn about the impostor syndrome back in 2009, around the time my first book was published. I was an academic staff member at the University of Wisconsin–La Crosse. After my book became popular with small-business owners, several of the UW campuses around the state asked me to teach a class at their respective campuses. Awesome. One day I mentioned this opportunity to a family friend: I told him I was headed to the University of Wisconsin–Green Bay the next day to teach a class based on my search engine optimization (SEO) book.

My friend looked at me and said, "Well, why are they having you teach the class? Couldn't they find someone in Green Bay to teach it?"

My friend was not trying to be hurtful—not in the least. But those comments hit me hard. Never mind that my SEO book was number 3 in the United States, or that I had just been interviewed for *Inc. Magazine*, or any of the other credibility indicators. When he asked me that question, I actually paused and thought about it. "Yeah, why are they hiring *me* to teach? Am I good enough? Do I have what it takes? Am I the best they could bring in? Do I deserve to be there? Am I a fraud? Do I even know what I'm talking about?"

There is nothing unique about my story. We have all had experiences where we begin to hear the voice in our heads whispering—or in some cases shouting—"Who do you think you are?"

The impostor syndrome will work hard to hold you back.

High performers with impostor syndrome may work obsessively to prevent people from discovering that they're "impostors." And talk about a vicious cycle: The hard work leads to more praise and success, which only perpetuates the impostor feelings, leading the "impostor" to work even harder, which can lead to sleep deprivation, burnout, and worse.

Ingredient #2: The "impostor" takes the proof of success and passes it off as luck, timing, or the result of deceiving others into thinking he or she is more intelligent and competent than the person believes.

Has your business ever gone through a growth spurt that you couldn't explain? Have you ever looked around your office and suddenly realized you have some amazing people working for you and looking to you for leadership—and, yet, you cannot figure out what they see in you? Have you ever felt uncomfortable before a presentation with a new client? Did you wonder why the client invited *you* to the table?

Why do we ask ourselves such lousy and unfair questions?

Here's the important point that I really want you to get. When you ask yourself, "How on earth were we able to hire such amazing employees? Don't they know that we don't know what in the world we're doing?" your brain does a funny thing . . . it gives you an answer.

It's a crummy answer but it's an answer. Your brain doesn't want to make you out to be a liar—so it gives you the answer to fit your story.

You start hearing things like, "Yeah, you really pulled the wool over their eyes on that one. Hope Becky doesn't figure it out—because if she leaves—then Tom is sure to leave the company, too." Or, "Why did client X invite us here? We don't really have a shot at winning this pitch, do we?"

The answer you get back might be something like, "Nope, we have no chance of winning—especially if they knew about all the mistakes we made just last week on client Z's account. We are lucky to have kept client Z; I hope X doesn't ask for references. Maybe we ought to back out of the process now."

What nonsense. You were invited into the evaluation process because you have a stellar network—perhaps stellar credentials—and you deserve to be at the table. The voice on your shoulder—the voice whispering in your ear—is the impostor syndrome.

And we all deal with it. It doesn't matter who you are thinking of right now. Tim Ferriss, bestselling author of *The 4-Hour Workweek*, has dealt with it. Joel Osteen has dealt with it. All of the incredible business leaders who grace the cover of *Entrepreneur* magazine deal with it. Every business owner—every political leader—every leader throughout history has dealt with this. George Washington did not feel he was worthy to be this country's first president. No one is immune from impostor syndrome.

But what is unique—and what is special—is when someone faces the fear of potential rejection. To quote the beautiful words of educator and behavior expert Dr. Marcie Beigel, a two-time *Onward Nation* guest, "Stephen . . . be scared, and then do it anyway!" I loved that.

Because it is oftentimes fear—which is another way of describing impostor syndrome—that gets in your way more than anything else. You may be your own biggest constraint. Not your ability to schedule guests on your show, not your ability to sell, not the market, not your lack of customers, not your pricing, not your product quality. No, it is you. You, as the owner, set the pace and tempo of your company: either fast or slow.

I asked Dr. Marcie to share how business owners can reach that elusive next level. She was kind enough to map it out in three simple steps:

1. Get clear on what the next level is—how will you know when you're there?
2. Walk through your fear; make a plan—and just do it.
3. Find a mentor—we learn best from the people who have been there.

And let's look at all three of these.

First, get clear on what the next level is for you and your business. Well, if impostor syndrome (aka fear) is making you believe that you are not even worthy of your current level of success, then how could you possibly believe you're worthy of being the host of a top-ranked podcast?

Great question, right? Instead, perhaps you need to spend some time being thankful for what you have already accomplished by consciously acknowledging that what you have achieved has been well deserved because you worked hard and you applied your God-given gifts and talents to get there.

Now, to realize your full potential, it's time to leap off your current plateau and move onward to that next level. You deserve to be at the next level. You're an expert. The first step is to give yourself permission to define that next level so you know when you, your podcast, and your business have arrived.

Second, be scared about the next level . . . and do it anyway. Kick fear to the curb. What's the worst that could happen? Prospective customers could say no. You might make a bad decision and lose some money. An employee or a group of employees may disagree with how you're redirecting the company and could decide to leave.

Okay. Are any of these life-threatening situations? Did anyone die? No? Then move on!

Stop making each decision more than it has to be. Just make a decision. Then move on. It doesn't have to be more complicated than that. As Dr. Marcie said, "Be scared and then do it anyway."

Finally, find a mentor to learn from, as Don Yaeger recommended in the Foreword of this book. More specifically, find a mentor or group of mentors who are all moving at a pace and tempo that is faster than you are. It matters who you spend your time with; if you spend your time with people who are moving at your current pace—or slower—those people may make you feel comfortable to be around, they may not challenge you, they may not push you or ask you tough questions, and it is easy to relax and unwind.

Why? Because as Coach John Wooden once said, "You will never outperform your inner circle." That's just human nature.

So you need to make sure the mentors you select are operating at a completely different level than you—a level to which you can reach and stretch. You want to get into a group of people where you don't currently belong and then work like crazy not to get left behind. In the process you'll expand and grow. You will then be able to leap from your current plateau onto the next rung.

As *Onward Nation* guest Scott McKain taught me, "Stephen, you cannot reach that next rung unless you are willing to let go of the current one you are hanging on to." Wise words.

You were meant for greatness. You are instilled with an infinite abundance of talent and gifts. Don't let something as small as fear limit all you were meant to be.

✓ **YOUR SUCCESS CHECKLIST** ✓

Proactively confront the three primary challenges you will face while embarking on production and launch of your podcast:

❑ How will my podcast make money and help grow my business? You need a clearly defined monetization strategy, and "I'm going to sell ads" isn't it.

❑ How much time will this take me? You must be able to invest at least four hours per month toward your podcast.

❑ How will I get guests? Defeating the impostor syndrome by following Dr. Marcie Beigel's three simple steps is your key to success. And they are:

1. Get clear on what the next level is—how will you know when you're there?
2. Walk through your fear; make a plan—and just do it.
3. Find a mentor—we learn best from the people who have been there.

And, lastly, follow the advice of Coach John Wooden and "protect your inner circle."

CHAPTER 2

TAKE YOUR VITALS

This chapter will help bring into focus what we at *Onward Nation* and Predictive ROI refer to as the *vital metrics* controlling the growth of a business. I learned the vital metrics principle directly from Darren Hardy, former publisher of *SUCCESS Magazine*. Darren, a former member of our Predictive ROI Board of Advisors, has been one of my most influential mentors in business.

Darren taught me how "vitals" represent a snapshot and oftentimes a visualization regarding the overall health of a business at any given moment. This chapter includes the comprehensive Evaluation of Predictive Success Metrics (EPSM) as a tool to complete later to provide a snapshot view of the sales and marketing "vitals" in any business. This evaluation will help diagnose any critical areas that may need attention before you receive an inflow of new leads and sales opportunities from your podcast or any proactive marketing system.

I met Darren when I was invited to attend one of his original High-Performance Forums held at Torrey Pines in La Jolla, California. I was one of twenty-three CEOs of fast-growth companies invited to spend two and a half days with Darren. We spent the time together working through the latest in sales and marketing strategies with some intense masterminding.

To say I was nervous would be an understatement. But by the time the weekend was over, Darren had accepted my invitation to speak at an upcoming live event Predictive ROI was hosting. Darren and I also worked out an agreement for him to join our board of advisers for twelve months, during which he would personally mentor me on growing our business and new directions we ought to consider. It was the most intense year of my business career and exactly what I needed to learn, even though the process was challenging and sometimes painful. A great mentor pushes even when the last thing you want is to be pushed.

Darren used a portion of the forum to teach all of us about the importance of our "success vitals." What were they? How to measure them? How to assess our current business health? The lessons I learned were so impactful and have added so much value into Predictive ROI and our ability to generate revenue from *Onward Nation* that I wanted to devote this chapter to sharing the most relevant insights.

At Darren's forum I met Don Yaeger, *New York Times* bestselling author, owner of three companies, outstanding man of faith, devoted husband, and one of the most rock star fathers I have seen in action. After that weekend Don and I became accountability partners, agreeing to call each other every Friday morning at seven thirty to report our Wins, Losses, AHAs, and Fixes. We have maintained that weekly accountability for nearly four years. In that time, Don has become one of my best friends and trusted advisers.

My hope is that this chapter will help bring into focus the vital metrics controlling the growth of a business. Your "vitals" represent a snapshot of your business's overall health at any given moment.

To assist in this process, I included our comprehensive Evaluation of Predictive Success Metrics (EPSM) as a tool for you to use. Your score will give you a quick view of the sales and marketing vitals in your business.

Why is your EPSM score important as it relates to launching your podcast? This evaluation will help you diagnose any critical areas that may need attention before your business is ready to properly handle an inflow of new leads and sales opportunities as a result of your podcast. In addition, your outcomes/score may indicate several corrective actions that need to be addressed so your podcast has the highest probability of success.

The corrective actions are also important because increasing the flow of leads and sales into an inefficient, ineffective, or absent system within your business is a recipe that could spell disaster. More companies go out of business from indigestion than from starvation. In other words, the problem is that there are too many opportunities, not too few. Having the right systems in place at the outset is essential to your long-term success.

Let's begin with several definitions to make sure we get the terminology right.

We will focus on vital priorities, vital functions, and vital metrics.

I will show you how to identify the five or six most relevant vital metrics for ensuring that your overall sales and marketing strategies are turning your business into what I like to call a "Sales-Generating Machine."

The first term we need to define is *vital priorities*. What are they and why are they . . . vital?

Let's think of vital priorities as your big goals over the next twelve months. If you were to accomplish nothing else, the year will still be a success because your vital priorities will have been checked off the list. On the other hand, if you don't accomplish these vital few, then other accomplishments won't really matter.

What are the vital priorities in your business right now?

Then there are the vital functions. These are the skills and the talents that make you the best person in your company at a certain set of tasks, processes, or projects. Vital functions are the tasks you cannot delegate and you cannot hire out. Not only are you good at them, but also you drive business growth by performing them.

Take a moment to consider your vital functions. What functions are critically important to the success of your business and cannot be delegated away? Resist the temptation to let yourself say things like: bookkeeping, answering the phone, emailing customers, preparing proposals, and a variety of other functions. Are all of those important? Yes. Are they vital? Yes. Can they be delegated? Yes!

What are you world class at? Or what could you be world class at if you dedicated the right amount of time and energy to it? What could you achieve world-class proficiency in that would move the business along a completely different trajectory? The answers are your vital functions.

Then there are the vital metrics. These metrics are how you will quantifiably measure your success toward accomplishing your vital priorities.

Before I share the vital metrics with you—let me try to preempt a question that tends to hook business owners and prevent them from moving forward. I am often asked, "Stephen, this sounds great but I have people on my team who are in charge of these metrics. Why do I need to care about these? I don't want to learn this stuff, and I certainly don't want this to become my vital function."

Excellent question. Consider this: You don't need to be the one who pulls the levers or turns the knobs. These metrics do not need to become your vital functions. But if you don't pay attention to them or care about them, no one else will either.

In my opinion, your Sales-Generating Podcast has six vital metrics that you need to monitor consistently:

1. Change (increase/decrease) in unique website visitors to your podcast's website
2. Change (increase/decrease) in conversion rate of unique website visitors into email opt-ins (list building to be used to increase size of audience/listeners to your podcast)
3. Change (increase/decrease) in conversion rate of guests into leads
4. Change (increase/decrease) in conversion rate of guest-leads into proposals
5. Change (increase/decrease) in conversion rate of guest-proposals into sales
6. Total podcast-related revenue and total business revenue

Are you currently tracking and monitoring vital metrics similar to these in your business? If you are, well done! You and your business may already be a superstar at growing revenue from your podcast strategy.

But if you're not already paying attention to these vital metrics, the resources in this book will help guide you through making the necessary adjustments so you can put precise checklists and ROI scorecards into place to ensure a regular rhythm of evaluation.

Evaluating Your Vitals

Are you ready to take your evaluation of your vitals even deeper? Figure 2-1 provides our comprehensive Evaluation of Predictive Success Metrics (EPSM) as a tool to provide a snapshot view of the sales and marketing "vitals" in any business. This evaluation will help diagnose any critical areas that may need attending to before new leads and sales opportunities flow into a business from your podcast.

Just answer the questions and then tally your score at the end.

FIGURE 2-1

Q1: Do you know the main reason your clients buy from you over your competitors?

_____ Don't know (0 points)   _____ Some (1 point)   _____ Yes (3 points)

Q2: Could you make a list with first name, last name, title, and company for your Dream 50 prospects?

_____ Don't know (0 points)   _____ Some (1 point)   _____ Yes (3 points)

Q3: Do you have a fixed budget or percentage of sales allocated to marketing?

_____ Don't know (0 points)   _____ Some (1 point)   _____ Yes (3 points)

Q4: Do you know your conversion rate of leads into clients: out of X number of leads, you get Y number of clients or sales that deliver $Z in profit?

_____ Don't know (0 points)   _____ Some (1 point)   _____ Yes (3 points)

Q5: Do you know the average cost to acquire a new client?

_____ Don't know (0 points)   _____ Some (1 point)   _____ Yes (3 points)

Q6: What is the average revenue that a client's initial sale/purchase represents for your business?

_____ Don't know (0 points)   _____ Some (1 point)   _____ Yes (3 points)

Q7: Do you have a nurturing content marketing system that delivers consistent communications that add value to your clients?

_____ Don't know (0 points)   _____ Some (1 point)   _____ Yes (3 points)

Q8: Does anyone on your team review Google Analytics data on a monthly basis and make proactive recommendations based on the findings?

_____ Don't know (0 points)   _____ Some (1 point)   _____ Yes (3 points)

Q9: If yes, does your Google Analytics account include conversion goals that track your opt-ins and lead gen?

_____ Don't know (0 points)   _____ Some (1 point)   _____ Yes (3 points)

Q10: Could you verbally articulate in two sentences or less what makes your company distinctive from any competitor?

_____ Don't know (0 points)   _____ Some (1 point)   _____ Yes (3 points)

Q11: Do you know what your annual rescission rate is with clients and why they stop buying from you?

_____ Don't know (0 points)　　_____ Some (1 point)　　_____ Yes (3 points)

Q12: Do you use a CRM like Infusionsoft, ACT!, Salesforce, Hubspot, or other platforms to act as the central repository for leads, prospect lists, and customer lists?

_____ Don't know (0 points)　　_____ Some (1 point)　　_____ Yes (3 points)

Q13: Do you actively use all the data mentioned above to target segments of prospects and customers in different ways for the various products or services you offer?

_____ Don't know (0 points)　　_____ Some (1 point)　　_____ Yes (3 points)

Q14: Do you know where your biggest source of untapped new business is and how to ultimately mine it?

_____ Don't know (0 points)　　_____ Some (1 point)　　_____ Yes (3 points)

Q15: How many client testimonials and success stories do you have?

_____ Don't know (0 points)　　_____ Some (1 point)　　_____ Yes (3 points)

Q16: Do you incorporate testimonials in all your marketing, advertising, and sales efforts?

_____ Don't know (0 points)　　_____ Some (1 point)　　_____ Yes (3 points)

Q17: Do you have experts in your industry who endorse you and your company?

_____ Don't know (0 points)　　_____ Some (1 point)　　_____ Yes (3 points)

Q18: Do you have any strategic alliances/joint venture relationships you are currently doing promotions with right now?

_____ Don't know (0 points)   _____ Some (1 point)   _____ Yes (3 points)

Q19: Do you know the lifetime value of a new client/customer?

_____ Don't know (0 points)   _____ Some (1 point)   _____ Yes (3 points)

Q20: Do you use a bold guarantee to create distinctiveness for your business?

_____ Don't know (0 points)   _____ Some (1 point)   _____ Yes (3 points)

Q21: Do you offer bonuses as an incentive to purchase your product or service?

_____ Don't know (0 points)   _____ Some (1 point)   _____ Yes (3 points)

Q22: Do you have an active PR program to do interviews on radio, on TV, in newspapers, or in magazines?

_____ Don't know (0 points)   _____ Some (1 point)   _____ Yes (3 points)

Q23: Do you use excerpts of these activities within your marketing?

_____ Don't know (0 points)   _____ Some (1 point)   _____ Yes (3 points)

Q24: Do you write articles, special reports, e-books, or books to share your expertise?

_____ Don't know (0 points)   _____ Some (1 point)   _____ Yes (3 points)

Q25: Do you have a strategy in place that continually adds new prospects into your database for your sales team to mine?

_____ Don't know (0 points)   _____ Some (1 point)   _____ Yes (3 points)

Q26: How often do you send relevant, content-rich emails delivering value to clients and prospects?

_____ Never (0 points)   _____ Twice per year (1 point)   _____ Every month (3 points)

Q27: Does your current website receive at least 60 percent of its traffic from organic search?

_____ Don't know (0 points)   _____ Some (1 point)   _____ Yes (3 points)

Q28: Do you hold, run, or host special events such as seminars or workshops where you invite clients and prospects to attend?

_____ Don't know (0 points)   _____ Some (1 point)   _____ Yes (3 points)

Q29: Do you personally talk to your buyers, prospects, and clients regularly to learn what they want and then build relationships with them?

_____ Don't know (0 points)   _____ Some (1 point)   _____ Yes (3 points)

Q30: Do you regularly shop your competitors to see what they do differently?

_____ Don't know (0 points)   _____ Some (1 point)   _____ Yes (3 points)

Q31: Do you know the Top 10 objections prospects have about your product or service?

_____ Don't know (0 points)   _____ Some (1 point)   _____ Yes (3 points)

Q32: Do you and your team know the answers to those Top 10 objections?

_____ Don't know (0 points)   _____ Some (1 point)   _____ Yes (3 points)

How Did You Do?

If you scored 33–50 . . . ugh. But no problem—this book will be a great guide for you.

If you scored 51–75 . . . congratulations. You have a solid foundation and the sky's the limit.

If you scored 76–85 . . . You feel that? It's *momentum*—and it feels awesome!

And if you scored 86–96 . . . rock solid awesome. You better send me an email (Stephen@onwardnation.com) because I want to interview you on *Onward Nation*! Well done.

Congratulations on your completion of the first two chapters in this book. Why am I offering you a congratulatory comment when there is still a lot left to learn and master?

Because most people will stop reading a book—any book—somewhere in the middle of Chapter 2. But you didn't stop! You are already ahead of the majority of your competitors. And if they stopped at Chapter 2, I can almost certainly guarantee they will not complete the work in the next chapters. You have already set yourself apart as a high achiever!

Now, are you ready to create, launch, promote, and monetize your very own podcast?

✓ YOUR VITALS CHECKLIST ✓

❑ Identify the vital priorities for your business, and your podcast, over the next twelve months. Ideally, the two lists will intersect.

❑ Identify your personal vital functions.

❑ Identify the baselines for the six vital metrics in this chapter so you can measure your impact in each area going forward.

❑ Complete the Evaluation of Predictive Success Metrics (EPSM) in this chapter to provide a snapshot view of the sales and marketing "vitals" in your business.

❑ Score your results and review with your team.

❑ Revise your list of vital priorities in order to immediately address each area highlighted from the EPSM.

CHAPTER 3

SYSTEM OVERVIEW— YOUR RECIPE FOR SUCCESS

> Analysis of several hundred people who had accumulated fortunes well beyond the million dollar mark disclosed the fact that every one of them had the habit of reaching decisions promptly, and of changing these decisions slowly, if, and when they were changed. People who fail to accumulate money, without exception, have the habit of reaching decisions, if at all, very slowly and of changing these decisions quickly and often.
>
> **–NAPOLEON HILL**[1]

Being successful at podcasting requires a variety of competencies and skills—all of which are covered in precise detail in this book. But the most important skills you must master in order to build a profitable podcast are making a decision, setting a course, and then remaining focused on moving toward your destination. Growing revenue, expanding your platform, and building a network of true fans through your podcast requires patience over a sustained period of time.

The Profitable Podcast System is not a get-rich-quick scheme. It's going to take hundreds of hours of your time to perfect your podcasting skills. But, this comprehensive resource will shorten your learning curve because you will be able to avoid the mistakes and reach profitability faster.

Your opportunity for success will increase if you keep Napoleon Hill's wise words front and center: Reach a decision quickly, be slow to change it, and relentlessly pursue your destination. Master this principle and you will create significant outcomes for your business as a result of the system offered in this book.

At a high level, the Profitable Podcast System includes twenty steps that stretch across multiple technical systems, software, and people, all of which must be properly coordinated and aligned with the desired outcomes. This chapter will provide you with a 30,000-foot view of the overall system before stepping deep into the weeds of strategy in the *7 Stages of Production*. The stages in the book will provide you with access to a complete tool kit of templates, guides, email swipe files, spreadsheets, schedules, and checklists to guide you every step of the way.

A few words of caution: As we move deeper into the system, it may begin to feel too complicated to integrate into your business. Yes, the system is complex, with many moving parts. However, rest assured, all the parts are not moving at the same time. The Profitable Podcast System is just like any other business system. It starts off seeming complex and confusing, but as time goes by you will develop mastery and nimbleness in making it all work for you.

At first, the system will feel a bit like trying to fly the space shuttle. There will be lots of "switches," "controls," "gauges," and "levers" inside the cockpit. But there is something very important to remember about flying the space shuttle. At any given time, there are only a couple of levers that need to be pulled—and a couple of buttons that need to be pushed. Everything else can be ignored.

The same principle applies here, too. Please don't get overwhelmed—don't get frustrated. Mastery will come.

I believe that the wise Archimedes had it right when he said, "Give me a lever and a place to stand and I will move the earth."

So, what will be your lever as you work through implementation and mastery of this system? You guessed it: chocolate cake!

I know, chocolate cake sounds silly. But let me explain why this metaphor makes so much sense for what you are about to learn.

Let's say that I happen to make the world's best chocolate cake—the absolute best. I have spent the last twenty years perfecting my process. Then one day you ask me to teach you how to make my cake—the one that took me twenty years to master!

How could this be possible? How could someone other than me even come close to duplicating my chocolate cake? Especially if you haven't dedicated yourself to mastering your baking skills as I have.

Is there something I could give you—to help prepare you—to help ensure your success? Well, I could give you my recipe, right?

If you have an opportunity to study and review my recipe, you'll see my full process—the strategy behind the chocolate cake. You'll begin to get the overall picture of what needs to happen.

But, what else do you need beyond the recipe? Exactly! You need the actual ingredients.

You can put it all together if you have access to the recipe (strategy) and the ingredients (tactics). You can see the entire project at a high level, especially if the recipe includes a photo of the finished cake. You have documentation regarding the right amount of each ingredient—at the right time—and how long to bake the cake at the right temperature.

If you follow the recipe—and if I didn't accidentally leave any steps or ingredients out of the recipe—you now have a decent shot at replicating my success.

In fact, replicating my success becomes easy *if* you are willing to make the effort and to put in the hard work. The cake won't bake itself. But you now have a clear path to follow. Just like this book will do for your podcast.

The system contains twenty core and interdependent steps:

- **Ingredient 1: Internal Kickoff Meeting.** You meet with your team to discuss production strategy, roles, prioritization, monetization goals, and vital metrics.
  - ‣ The kickoff meeting is where you and your team will get specific about your goals, vital metrics, discussing the avatar of your ideal prospect and customer, as well as the avatar of your prospective

listener. This is where you will name your show, crystalize how the show will drive leads and revenue for your business, and assemble your Dream 50 list of prospects, which represents the clients you would most like to serve in your industry.

▸ Your list of Dream 50 prospects will serve as the guest list for your podcast along with subject matter experts from a variety of relevant and complementary fields such as C-suite executives, business leaders, and other noncompetitive thought leaders.

▸ You will want to prioritize the selection of guests so your podcast can achieve the shortest path to revenue.

■ *Ingredient 2: Question Flow.* This is where you and your team will collaborate to prepare the preliminary question set for review and critique. Then create the final version, which will become the Question Flow used with guests on the show.

■ *Ingredient 3: Guest Advocacy System.* This is where you will implement our top-rated Guest Advocacy System, which includes setting up an online scheduling system, calendar integration, creation of interview reminders to guests, and the preparation of equipment recommendations for guests. All of the templates and resources you need for Guest Advocacy have been included in the book.

■ *Ingredient 4: Guest Invitations.* This is where you and your team will collaborate to create and finalize a guest invitation email with links to the online scheduling system. Again, a template has been provided.

■ *Ingredient 5: Invite Distribution.* This is where you, as the host of the podcast, will send the invitation emails to prospective guests and answer questions if necessary (this step initiates high-level dialogue with your Dream 50).

■ *Ingredient 6: Intro/Outro Scripted.* This is where you and your team will want to collaborate to create the script for your show's recorded intro and outro. Organizing your thoughts, and being organized, will save you time and money when it comes time to work with a producer on recording your intro and outro.

- ■ *Ingredient 7: Audio Production.* This is where you will want to connect with an audio producer to create the intro and outro for your show.

- ■ *Ingredient 8: Show Artwork.* This is where you will want to connect with a graphic designer, either on your team or a freelancer, to create your show artwork/thumbnail images for iTunes, Stitcher, website assets, etc. All design guidelines have been included in the book.

- ■ *Ingredient 9: Podcast Website.* You and your team should consider creating a website for your show. The website will serve as the podcast's headquarters complete with podcast player, social media plug-ins, and hosting (www.on-wardnation.com as example).

- ■ *Ingredient 10: Podcast Hosting.* There are a number of providers to choose from with respect to hosting the audio files for your show. However, Libsyn is an industry leader and my Predictive ROI team has never experienced a problem with the company. This is where you will create your hosting account, including show description, details for iTunes, Stitcher, Google Play, and RSS feed.

- ■ *Ingredient 11: Show Notes.* This is where you will create your Show Notes template for your podcast so that each episode will have its own blog post with the embedded audio file ready for your website visitors.

- ■ *Ingredient 12: iTunes.* This is where you will set up your podcast in iTunes.

- ■ *Ingredient 13: Stitcher.* This is where you will set up your podcast in Stitcher.

- ■ *Ingredient 14: Google Play.* This is where you will set up your podcast in Google Play.

- ■ *Ingredient 15: Airing Schedule.* Following the template in the book, you will be able to create and maintain your own Show Airing Schedule complete with show titles, production schedule, airing dates, Show Notes links, and other logistics.

- ***Ingredient 16: Audio Editing and Episode Airing.*** This is where learning all things audio will pay off—editing your actual episodes. This book includes a complete audio production guide. You will likely want to air at least one new episode per week so your audience can see that you are serious and you can begin to build your nation of true fans. You will want to provide your guests with email reminders, social media distribution, and promotional links so they can help spread the word of your great show.

- ***Ingredient 17: Launch Day.*** This is where you and your team will want to follow our launch recipe so you can dominate iTunes in your respective categories immediately upon launch of the podcast. For example, we recently assisted one of our Predictive ROI clients in reaching the top of iTunes. The show was ranked the number 1 podcast in Management and Marketing, number 2 in Education, number 2 in Careers, number 3 in Business, and the number 10 podcast in all of iTunes.

- ***Ingredient 18: Social Engagement with Guests.*** This is where you will want to follow our recipe for creating Facebook, LinkedIn, and Twitter posts to promote each episode. We have a unique social media recipe that will warm up your guests for your sales opportunity that systematically shares their expertise from the episode. For example, you will learn how to create a library of ten tweets per episode. Each tweet will share valuable highlights from the episode and include the Twitter handle of the guest who contributed the highlight. The library of tweets will be auto-distributed at random on a regular schedule. This encourages guests to re-tweet their episode to their respective followers. Examples of social media posts have been provided in Chapter 4, "Grow Your Revenue."

- ***Ingredient 19: iTunes What's Hot Rank Continuity.*** After eight weeks, your podcast will fall out of iTunes' New and Noteworthy rankings and move into What's Hot. You should follow our recipe for keeping a steady stream of ratings and reviews flowing into iTunes. This will keep your organic downloads as high as possible.

- ***Ingredient 20: Continuous Review of Vital Metrics.*** Schedule a tactical Checkpoint Meeting with your team every fourteen days to ensure that the podcast is running smoothly and to review/revise/expand the Dream 50 list, review feedback from guests, etc. And schedule an ROI Scorecard Meeting every thirty days to evaluate vital metrics including lead gen success and to discuss adjustments.

Timing and Expectations

We went from zero to launch in thirty days when *Onward Nation* went live on June 15, 2015. It's possible for you and your team to follow the recipe in this book and replicate our timeline. However, based on our experience in creating, launching, and producing more than fifty podcasts for Predictive ROI clients, I recommend you and your team give yourselves between seven and eight weeks to go from zero to launch.

CHAPTER 4

GROW
YOUR REVENUE

When executed properly, your podcast will be uniquely suited to accomplish three *vital priorities*: grow revenue, expand your platform, and build a nation of true fans. The next three chapters will provide you with the specific recipes and ingredients you need to accomplish all three. The recipes build upon one another—but the recipes are also "interdependent." As the late Stephen R. Covey wrote in *The 7 Habits of Highly Effective People*, with interdependence, "you and I working together can accomplish far more than, even at my best, I could accomplish alone." The next three chapters are interdependent because they work in unison, and together they create synergistic momentum for your business. As your platform grows, so will your nation of true fans, and as your nation grows, so will your opportunity to further grow the revenue of your business.

Your opportunity to grow revenue will likely fit into three primary categories:

- Premium-priced services to the business owners who have appeared as guests on your show
- Less expensive, entry-level programs to your concentric circles of lesser fans (see Chapter 6 for lesser fans)
- Sponsorships to boost revenue and credibility with your listeners (see Chapter 16)

In my opinion, you will have a healthy core business if selling your services directly to your guests represents the majority of your podcast-related revenue. This sales strategy will ensure that there is ample revenue flowing into your core business to cover overhead, generate profit, provide ample funds to reinvest, and further expand by introducing new services to continue the life cycle of a balanced business. It is important for your podcast to feed your core business. It is also important for you not to become distracted with creating a passive revenue income as your first step. Passive revenue streams can be helpful and provide high-margin sources of revenue. However, it can sometimes be tempting to want to create a passive revenue stream first because it feels less like selling. Wouldn't it be wonderful to wake up each morning and see all of the successful credit card transaction receipts in your in-box? Of course it would. But not at the expense of your core team not having enough work to do. If you pursue the goal of creating a passive revenue stream for your business—before you address the lead gen and revenue needs of your core business—you run the risk of losing valuable time and getting sidetracked. And that could be expensive.

Rather than devoting a section of this chapter to a passive revenue recipe, I have included our complete recipe including several promotional launch plans as a free download at http://PredictiveROI.com/Resources/Passive-Revenue.

Let's focus our attention back to your guests. You will maximize your revenue opportunity, and ensure the health of your core business, if you quickly begin using your podcast as your Trojan horse of selling as we discussed in the Introduction of this book.

Selling directly to your guests represents your lowest hanging fruit, your shortest path to revenue, and it is not a complex sales strategy. It could be as simple as sharing ideas with a guest following your interview, in an informal manner, looping back to the guest after you flesh out the ideas further, and then asking for permission to proceed. Lee Caraher, host of the *Focus Is Your Friend* podcast, shared her sales strategy with me.

Stephen, there's usually fifteen minutes before we start the interview where I say, "Oh my gosh, hi. Blah, blah, blah." Then afterwards, I am sharing with them, "I have an idea for you," which is where I'm really good. That's one of my strengths. "Oh, here's an idea! Or, here's a different idea!" I share the ideas after the interview is over. Depending on how my guest reacts, if they say, "Oh that'd be a great idea. How do I do that?" Then I say, "Let me think about it some more."

A week or two later, I'll noodle on the idea a little more. Then I'll email them with, "You know, I thought about that idea. Here is how I think you could implement it. Here is what I think the lift will be. Here is what I think the cost will be. We can't do that for you—or—we can do that for you." Of that, 25 percent of the time the ideas are coming back to us in some sort of project. Our podcast been super helpful in growing revenue for Double Forte.

Ingredient #1: The Campfire Pitch

Lee has developed a straightforward sales strategy. Her podcast opened the door with the right decision-maker, she conducted a rock-solid interview, and then she enthusiastically shared ideas with her guest. I call this the *Campfire Pitch*.

When you were a kid, did you ever go camping with family or friends, or have a bonfire in your backyard? Maybe you sat around the fire, feeling warm, and sharing stories with your friends. The energy of the group was awesome. But then the party was over, it was time for bed, and when you woke up the next morning, the same people were with you but the energy of the moment was gone. That's what entrepreneur and brand expert Chris Smith calls the *Campfire Effect*. It happens in business—after a great interview, for example—and it happens in social situations.

Lee knows this and has astutely aligned her sales strategy to the Campfire Effect. When the energy of the interview has climaxed, she smartly shares an idea or two. The prospective client (guest) on the other end of the Skype connection is receptive to the ideas because of several key ingredients: For one thing, Lee is brilliant at what she does and she is sharing excellent ideas. Also, the guest is receptive because of the Campfire Effect and the value Lee has just shared by inviting the client onto her show.

Lee is airing approximately fifty to seventy guest interviews per year—so if her team continues to close 25 percent of the opportunities, then her podcast will help Double Forte on-board approximately fifteen new projects every twelve months. Think about that in terms of your core business and revenue model. If you could take on fifteen new projects from clients within the next twelve months, how would your business change? No doubt it is substantial.

One of the reasons Lee has been successful with her Campfire Pitch sales strategy is because she doesn't approach the conversations with her guests as selling at all. She enthusiastically shares ideas with the goal of delivering value. One *Onward Nation* guest told me, "*Selling is simply the transference of your enthusiasm over to your prospect.*" Lee has mastered this principle. Her guests don't feel "sold." In fact, the exact opposite happens: They feel fortunate to have had the opportunity to be a guest on her show. Lee's ideas were a value-added bonus.

Ingredient #2: The Social Media Warm-Up

The Campfire Pitch Lee Caraher uses is masterful. But, I also realize it might not be for everyone because not everyone feels comfortable about sharing ideas and selling so early in the relationship. I respect that. So I wanted to share a second sales strategy with you. We call it the *Social Media Warm-Up*.

The Social Media Warm-Up sales strategy is already baked into the overall recipe of your *Profitable Podcast*. In Chapter 11, you will learn how to promote the airing of each of your guest's episodes via social media using two key ingredients:

- Promoting the airing of each episode and the wisdom shared by your guest to your social media community.
- Tagging your guests in each post whenever possible so they are nudged to share and re-tweet your content. This helps build your nation of true fans by exposing their community to your content.

But your social media strategy does more than help you promote your episodes and build your nation. By highlighting your guest's wisdom in each tweet, and by tagging the guest, you are continually reminding your guests of the value they shared with your community. This makes your guests feel good—and rightly so. After all, they delivered massive value—you recognized that—and you are now shouting it from the rooftops. By doing so, you are continually stoking the Campfire Effect with each of your guests.

With some of your guests, the fire will begin burning hot so that when you reach back out to them to discuss how your core business might be able to help their business, one of the first things they may say to you at the onset of the call is, "Thanks for all of the tweets!" Then you will know that your Social Media Warm-Up opened the door exactly as you intended. I always smile when it happens. Rock-solid awesome!

However, there's a key ingredient missing, isn't there? How should you reach back out to your guests to reopen the door, tee up the potential sales opportunity, and then schedule the call to discuss? I am going to share the "door-opening email" we developed at Predictive ROI so you can revise the content to match your business model and sales process.

Figure 4-1 is a screenshot of the email responsible for opening the door to $2 million of revenue flowing into Predictive ROI over the next twelve months. The recipients of the email are *Onward Nation* guests. *Onward Nation* is our daily podcast for business owners, but my core business, Predictive ROI, is a content marketing and lead generation agency.

FIGURE 4-1

Good Evening Lee . . . hope all is well with you, my friend. Thank you again for sharing your wisdom and expertise during **Episode 180 of *Onward Nation*!**

I really appreciate it. Would love to have you back for an ENCORE! Just let me know.

Wanted to share some exciting news . . .

Recently . . . our team tested the waters to see if we could produce multiple podcasts simultaneously.

It worked—and—we perfected our *iTunes Marketing Strategy* in the process.

For example . . . we launched the **Business Rescue Road Map podcast with Stacy Tuschl**—and—she became the ***#1 ranked podcast in her iTunes category in just 48-hours***.

So we took a deep breath . . . carefully reviewed our system . . . liked what we saw . . . and began to privately introduce our ***Sales Generating Podcast System*** to some friends of *Onward Nation*.

It is now a complete done-for-you podcasting and sales generating system.

Our system will help you:

- Build relationships with your dream prospects
- Deliver high-quality content consistently to your audience
- Leverage your thought leadership to further grow your audience
- And most importantly—it will accelerate your leads and sales

It would be an honor to talk with you about how we might be able to do the same for you.

We are sharing this with a small group of friends—including special pricing—until June 1st.

I'd love to talk with you about it.

Would you have time one day next week for a brief call?

Onward with gusto!

Stephen Woessner
Host of the *Onward Nation* Podcast
CEO of Predictive ROI
M: 608-498-5165

One Predictive ROI core service is helping owners of business-to-business professional services firms create and launch their own podcasts so they can grow revenue, expand their platform, and build a nation of true fans. So it seems reasonable that if a business owner was comfortable enough to be my guest on *Onward Nation*, then there may be some interest on behalf of some guests to have their own podcast, which is exactly what has happened.

Let's walk through a tangible example. When Lee Caraher was my guest on *Onward Nation*, she crushed it. Wow. We had an incredible conversation so it was easy to see that Lee would be an incredible host if she had her own podcast. We aired on February 26, 2016. In March, April, and May we had no openings. Our production capacity was full because we had just on-boarded several new podcasting clients. But around mid-May we could begin to forecast availability in June. My team and I also wanted to increase our pricing to improve our margins.

So, I began reaching out to more *Onward Nation* guests to gauge interest in two things: Would they like to come back for an encore interview? And would they like to have a conversation about how our podcasting system might deliver value to their businesses?

I sent the email in Figure 4-1 to Lee on Sunday, May 15, 2016. She got back to me the next day with the email you see in Figure 4-2. Lee and her team move at an uncommon pace, so we swiftly scheduled a brief call to consider the opportunity.

FIGURE 4-2

Hi Stephen—good to hear from you.

1. I'd love to return to your show—I think I mentioned my next book comes out next April—can we schedule this in conjunction with this rollout? This fall or early next year—unless of course you want me 3 times!!!

2. I'd love to talk with you more about your podcast biz—I'm ccing my colleague Liz O'Donnell here who is in charge of making our podcast a reality—I'd like to have her on the phone too—ok?

3. Ccing David here to help with scheduling

Thanks
Have a great day
Lee

SAN FRANCISCO | BOSTON | NEW YORK
Lee McEnany Caraher | President & CEO
T: 415.500.0602 | M:650.302.3457
Twitter: @leecaraher |@DoubleFortePR
E: lcaraher@double-forte.com | W: double-forte.com

Meanwhile, I worked with Lee's assistant to schedule the encore interview, which took place at the end of June. When Lee and I connected, she let me know they were just a few days away from making a final decision about their own podcast. Awesome.

And as promised, she looped back to me with her project approval before our new pricing strategy went into effect.

The Social Media Warm-Up is an efficient sales process for three key reasons:

+ *Onward Nation* guests are successful leaders and business owners in their industries, so they can fund a program like what we are offering.

- We provided an exceptional experience for them as guests on our show and now they have the opportunity to put that same system into place for their businesses.
- We stoked the Campfire Effect via social media and shared the wisdom and expertise from their *Onward Nation* episodes with our ever-growing community.

All of which equals significant value leading into the sales process.

Before we close out this chapter, I want to offer some important words of caution. The Campfire Pitch and Social Media Warm-Up sales strategies are simple to execute, simple to measure (you either sold something or you didn't), and simple to adjust and modify. Plus, they produce results quickly. But don't let the simplicity fool you. Some business owners think the strategies are too simple to be effective. "How can these strategies deliver results without having to rely on complex systems or software?" Then the business owners go down the path of creating databases, marketing automation tools, landing pages, webinars, and a variety of other systems instead of concentrating on the vital priorities right in front of them.

Don't let this be you.

Your podcast is your Trojan horse of sales. The sales strategies do not have to be complicated. Keep them simple. And by doing so, you will grow your revenue.

✓ SALES STRATEGY CHECKLIST ✓

❏ Have you crafted your monetization strategy? Remember, "I'm going to sell ads" likely isn't it.

❏ Have you completed the EPSM found in Chapter 2? If not, go back and complete this step because it will be extremely challenging to succeed in generating new leads and revenue if your current vital metrics are askew.

❏ You and your team should review the twenty steps in the launch process outlined in Chapter 3 and then decide who will accomplish what vital function.

❏ Decide if the Campfire Pitch or the Social Media Warm-Up will become your sales strategy.

CHAPTER 5

EXPAND
YOUR PLATFORM

I n my opinion, there are two sides to expanding your platform. There is the technical nuts and bolts side, which we will cover in this book's production-related chapters. There is also the content side, which we will cover in this chapter. The quality of your content, and your intention for creating the content in the first place, are key ingredients in determining your ability to expand your platform. Expanding your platform is not about spending large amounts of money on Facebook campaigns, buying email lists, running Google AdWords campaigns, or investing in the myriad other ways you could buy traffic to your website. Instead, it's about having an intentional strategy for creating and delivering valuable content to your audience (your nation!) in such a way that a relationship is formed with an audience who loves you and what your platform represents.

Expanding your platform through your podcast will give you the opportunity to attract an audience who will ultimately become your nation of true fans

(Chapter 6) if you execute and expand properly. The more and better-qualified traffic flowing into your platform, the better your revenue opportunity will be.

This chapter will take you through the definition of what a platform is, why expanding your platform matters to your business and your audience, and how your podcast represents an excellent content marketing and platform expansion opportunity all rolled into one.

Let's begin by defining the term *platform*. My good friend Wendy Keller is the author of the brilliant book *Ultimate Guide to Platform Building*. In it, she shares a practical and tactical definition for *platform* that in my opinion is spot on for every business owner:

Platform = traffic

Traffic = money

Therefore, platform = money

Get a platform, get money

Wendy also shares several helpful criteria I recommend you consider as you evaluate whether to expand your platform:

- You want to grow your business by attracting new customers and clients.
- You have a new business you are trying to launch.
- Your sales are slumping—or never got off the ground.
- You want to introduce a product or service to the market.
- You would like to attract investors or partners.
- You yearn to expand your brand.
- You are searching for new streams of revenue.
- You want to distinguish your career.
- You are being eaten alive by the competition.
- You are a speaker, coach, or consultant (or want to be) and you are putting your game plan together.
- You just want to make more money.

I suspect most business owners who review Wendy's criteria would agree that expanding their platform as a means to achieving all or a portion of that list would be a worthy pursuit. So to take this platform discussion deeper, I sat down with Drew McLellan, top dog at the Agency Management Institute and host of the podcast *Build a Better Agency*. Drew is also a three-time alum on *Onward Nation*. (If you go to OnwardNation.com and type the word *Drew* into our search bar, all of his episodes will appear so you can listen.)

During his third visit, I asked Drew to share more about why a business owner ought to build a platform as a means to serve and add value to others, not just to drive financial results—and why a person's intention should come from the right place. Here's what Drew had to say. It's masterful.

Any platform I have, whether it's a blog or if I'm speaking, and certainly the podcast is one of my critical platforms, but for me every platform should be a place where I am being helpful, where I am using my expertise, my connection, my experiences to teach someone how to do something better. Ultimately that's really the whole point of Agency Management Institute— helping people run their businesses better. That's very much my mindset; plus, when you think about all of the information that's out there in all of the different platforms, blogs, webinars, podcasts, videos, or whatever it is, it's not like people don't have choices. So why in the world would they choose to give you their time over someone else?

They're only going to do that if (A) you're super entertaining, which I'm not. Or (B), you are helpful and you add value so that hour is an investment on their part where they get more out of the hour than it costs them to give you the hour, or whatever the time of consumption is.

When I add that kind of value and when I stay super focused on delivering, it comes back to me business-wise in spades. In marketing we often talk about how it is whoever is trying to sell something who is the one who has to provide value first so you have to sort of demonstrate your commitment to the audience.

You have to help them get where they want to go so that they can know, like, and trust you. Really that's what platform building is about. Giving people an opportunity to get to know you and over time because, as your listeners have experienced, they do get a sense of who you are and what you are about.

So for some listeners they gravitate toward that, and they, like you and other listeners probably on my podcast, go, for whatever reason, "I don't really love him so I'm going to stop listening." After you get through the know and like, then over time when you consistently deliver value and good advice and good counsel, then they become ready to trust you and when they're ready to trust you, not only does that mean that they will keep consuming my content. It also means that they are going to be open to an AMI workshop or one of the other things that we do that we actually make money at. It's all part of a continuum, I think.

Ultimately, you're doing it for a business purpose, but I think you're doing it with integrity. I always want my clients to feel like they get more from me than they give me, whether it's money, or time, or whatever. I'm modeling that all the way through my content creation. I always want to give more than somebody is in essence paying for because then whatever I'm charging them feels like a bargain and to them it is a bargain; the value proposition and the value transfer falls in their favor. To me that's smart business and so, yes, I'm doing it because it builds my business but I know that probably 90 percent of, for example, my podcast audience may or may not ever buy anything from me and that's fine.

A lot of my current customers who were customers before I started the podcast are avid podcast listeners, so now that's added value for them. Because they're part of the AMI family they knew about the podcast and they listen and for them that's like bonus value. For somebody who's never bought anything from us or doesn't know who I am, or doesn't know how we can help their agency, this is a way for us to introduce ourselves.

The other reason why I think everybody should have a platform is because especially when you sell something and you say you're an expert in something, saying you're an expert is one thing, demonstrating week after week that you're an expert is a completely different gig.

Again, it's critically important for you to understand that your skill in expanding your platform is not about mastering tech but about building a relationship with your audience. And that relationship deepens based on the value of the content you deliver on a consistent basis. The value of the content you deliver is high when your intention is in the right place. Your audience will know if you are solely focused on conversion rates and revenue. Consequently, you will not grow your revenue and you will likely fall short of your goals.

Earlier in this chapter, I mentioned that your podcast represents an excellent content marketing and platform expansion opportunity all rolled into one. I am going to share several content marketing ingredients you should consider, but first, let's bring in Joe Pulizzi, founder of the Content Marketing Institute (CMI), to define content marketing. CMI defines content marketing as "the practice of creating relevant and compelling content in a consistent fashion to a targeted buyer, focusing on all stages of the buying process, from brand awareness through to brand evangelism."[1]

Joe and his team at CMI have been the leaders in content marketing education and training for nearly a decade. This chapter is not intended to make you a content marketing expert. Instead, it will provide you with several tangible examples so you can see how you can get more value and content distribution mileage out of your episodes beyond just an audio file that's available for download inside iTunes.

Ingredient #1: Build Your Email List

One of the best ways to build your email list is by offering visitors to your podcast website what I like to call a "screaming cool value exchange," or a freemium. Something your website visitors consider to be so amazingly awesome and valuable that, when they see it, they exclaim to themselves, "Heck yeah, I want that," and happily share their email address with you to get it. You will know you have the value proposition correct when between 6 and 13 percent of your website visitors opt in to get their hands on your value exchange.

Ingredient #2: Increase Organic Search Traffic to Your Podcast Website

Google loves content pages that are at least 500 words in length but typically not longer than 1,000 words. An efficient way to boost word count to your Show Notes pages (Show Notes are covered in detail in Chapter 12) is to add the full or partial transcript below the Show Notes for each episode—and then optimize the entire page for search.

Ingredient #3: Put Podcast Interviews on Your YouTube Channel

Lewis Howes is a business owner who has mastered all three vital priorities in this book: growing revenue, expanding the platform, and building a nation of true fans. When Lewis talks strategy and execution, I really pay attention. Recently he began to conduct his podcast interviews on video in his studio and then air the content as a video on his YouTube channel before sending the audio-only version out to iTunes, Stitcher, Google Play, etc. as a traditional podcast. It's a smart strategy for creating compelling and valuable content for your nation of true fans. You can find Lewis on YouTube here: https://www.youtube.com/user/lewishowes.

Ingredient #4: Turn Your Audio into Video

Kinetic typography is an outstanding visual strategy for converting short snippets of audio into video that can be shared on YouTube, Facebook, or other social media. The downside is that the time investment to create the typography is significant. For example, if you go to http://bit.ly/2eHJD7d you will see a short clip that my team produced following my guest appearance on *EOFire* with John Lee Dumas. This clip took about forty hours to produce, but it created an interesting twist on the lesson I shared during the interview with JLD.

Ingredient #5: Send Weekly Emails to Your Nation of Fans

Not everyone in your audience (your nation of true fans) will download and listen to every podcast episode as soon as it airs. Sending a weekly email summary of the highlights is an excellent way to keep your audience engaged and informed. You will also begin to build a reputation as a valuable curator of high-quality content. Kelly Hatfield, host of the *Absolute Advantage Podcast*, sends a weekly email similar to what is shown in Figure 5-1. Within the first several weeks of sending the emails, one of Kelly's Dream 50 prospects replied with a new business opportunity for Kelly and her firm. They successfully closed the deal, and the project generated nearly immediate ROI for the investment Kelly had made in launching her podcast. Rock-solid awesome!

FIGURE 5-1

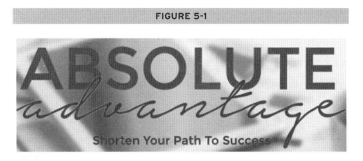

Good Morning Stephen,

Last week, I shared with you a powerful lesson from one of my recent guests on our new podcast called *Absolute Advantage*.

Today I'm going to share with you a lesson I learned from my guest on yesterday's episode, Kute Blackson. He is an absolute rockstar -- and -- this lesson will help you *shorten your path to success*.

Kute said to me...

"Before you lead someone else -- before you try and tell people what to do -- you have to lead yourself. If you can't get yourself to do the basics -- then how do you have inner integrity with yourself? When you have that integrity, your words have power."

Stephen, we are hit with messages every day about how crucial being a leader is for achieving the success we desire. But being a leader comes with requirements.

You don't simply become a leader by calling yourself one. You become a leader by leading -- and -- that starts with leading yourself first.

Go here to listen to my full interview with Kute Blackson.

Until next week...here's to *shortening your path to success!*

Kelly Hatfield

425.374.0182

Ingredient #6: Write Your Book with Your Podcast Episodes

Writing a book tends to be a common aspiration of most business owners, but the thought of investing all of the hours toward writing the book seems incomprehensible to be able to fit into one's schedule. Is writing a book one of your vital priorities? If so, I encourage you to let your podcast create all of the content for you. *Onward Nation* guest John Livesay did exactly that. He had ten of the best interviews from his *The Successful Pitch* podcast transcribed, then he edited them into chapters, and they became the core chapters of his book, *The Successful Pitch: Conversations About Going from Invisible to Investable.*

These six ingredients represent a small sampling of content marketing strategies you can employ to leverage each of your podcast episodes into more value for your audience and a platform expansion for your business!

✓ YOUR PLATFORM EXPANSION CHECKLIST ✓

- ❑ Build your email list.

- ❑ Increase organic search traffic to your podcast website.

- ❑ Put podcast interviews on your YouTube channel.

- ❑ Turn your audio into video.

- ❑ Send weekly emails to your nation of fans.

- ❑ Write your book with your podcast episodes.

CHAPTER 6

BUILD YOUR NATION
OF TRUE FANS

Downloaded more than 100,000 times, *Onward Nation* has listeners in nearly 200 countries around the world. These metrics are gratifying to my team and myself. I feel blessed and honored to have the opportunity to do what we love to do.

However, these metrics—as fun as they are to see in a data dashboard—do not represent the true economic engine behind *Onward Nation*, just as the number of countries, downloads, etc., will likely not represent a driving force of revenue into your business either. Instead, the way your podcast can potentially generate millions of dollars in new revenue is through creating and nurturing long-term relationships with your podcast guests. These relationships are what *Wired* magazine founder Kevin Kelly calls "True Fans."[1] True fans represent your ROI Scorecard's ultimate vital metric.

To paraphrase Kelly, any business owner can create a solid revenue stream around a community of approximately 1,000 people when they are "True Fans" of what the company sells and when there is a connection between the company and its fans based on the value provided. This chapter will illustrate how a consistent effort toward the production of your podcast can create a nation of true fans for your company.

Even if you didn't generate any direct or indirect revenue from your listeners through advertising, sponsorships, or offering up programs for sales— and focused only on converting guests into clients—you would reach 1,000 true fans in just three and a half years by airing one new episode per day. *Onward Nation* is already halfway there; in less than two years of airing, our podcast has generated approximately $2 million in revenue for Predictive ROI over twelve months.

The tactical steps for accomplishing this result were covered in detail in Chapter 4. But the outcome would not be possible if we had not invested the time—and continue to invest the time—to build a nation of fans who share their insights on how we can continually improve and move onward to that next level.

Your nation of true fans will be fans of you, fans of your message, and fans of your business. Your fans will support you because of the sacred bond you have built with them and because you consistently delivered massive value through your podcast content.

Whether you air a new episode every day or every week, no matter what airing schedule you decide upon, no matter the rhythm, the fact that you are consistent is the critical piece.

Now, let's get dialed in on building your nation of true fans: a sense of community, collaboration, and profitability around the purpose of your business.

We'll begin by breaking down the phrase "Build a nation of true fans" into its three core components: (1) Build, (2) Nation, and (3) True Fans.

Ingredient #1: Build (as in Your Platform—See Chapter 5)

How would you begin to "Build" a nation of true fans? You'd begin with a platform, such as:

- Podcast
- Speaking
- Blog
- YouTube channel/vlog
- Instagram stories
- Facebook Live

The platform you choose is irrelevant from a tech perspective. Any or all of the above can help you build a nation of true fans. The tech behind it is relatively easy. Is there a learning curve? Sure there is. Will you at times feel like you are trying to fly the space shuttle, as I mentioned in Chapter 3? Sure. How does Facebook Live work? What time of day should I create a story on Instagram? What kind of camera and microphone are best if I want to become a serious YouTuber?

All of these are tech questions that can be answered in an afternoon with your old friend Google. You can solve those problems and find the answers as long as you don't let the fear of the unknown paralyze you.

So, let's shift our focus away from the tech and toward the value you will be providing through those channels. What's your story? How will you serve your audience? How will you make what you are doing so valuable to their businesses or their lives that they actually consider you indispensable?

How will you become so consistent in over-delivering help, advice, recommendations, and value that you begin to build deposits in their emotional bank accounts, that your guests and your audience trust you, and then like you, and then get even closer as they begin to actually know you?

Your first step in building your nation of true fans has nothing to do with the actual content delivery platform, and everything to do with the value of what you will be delivering, because your nation of true fans is built on *value*. And if you get that recipe right, then the actual platform, or the "conduit" through which you share and distribute your value, will fall into place. The entire process will begin to feel less stressful because the value you were called to create and deliver will then be in the driver's seat. You will become unstoppable.

Ingredient #2: Nation

Now let's shift our attention to the word *nation* and break that down. And I want to make sure we address this because we live in a world where bigger lists, bigger subscribers, massive downloads, huge customer lists, etc., etc., etc., are what attract headlines and massive attention.

You don't need an email list of 100,000 people to build your nation. You don't need to have a podcast that gets a million downloads a month. You don't need to have a list of 20,000 prospects.

Nope. You don't.

That's not your nation.

What you need—depending on the size of your business—is somewhere between 100 and 1,000 highly qualified prospects. In fact, your knowledge with some of your prospects should be so deep that you can boldly claim them as your Dream 50 prospects.

If you need a refresher on why your Dream 50 matter, you can go to Chapter 7, where I map it all out: how to figure out who your Dream 50 are and how to romance your Dream 50 so they understand how important they are to you.

To take this point deeper, I want to share a tangible example of a company that grew from zero to a multi-billion-dollar-a-year business. Yes, *billion* with a capital *B*.

Earlier, I mentioned my mentor, Darren Hardy, former publisher of *SUCCESS Magazine*. A while back, he decided to interview my friend Cody Foster, cofounder of Advisors Excel, and share the interview on the March 2014 edition of the *SUCCESS CD* that rides along with the magazine.

During the interview with Darren, Cody shared several personal stories of very humble beginnings—stories that helped shape the kind of company Advisors Excel has become.

Advisors Excel is packed full of incredible people. The team's sole aim is to deliver more and more value every day to financial advisers around the country. The Advisors Excel team does it masterfully well. They built their platform on a solid foundation of value.

But, did they build this platform by trying to serve the 60,000 financial advisers located in the state of Florida alone? No. How about all of the financial advisers up and down the West Coast? Nope.

Did they focus on spending large amounts of advertising dollars trying to reach everyone they could with their message of value, value, value? Not at all.

Instead, they meticulously selected 1,000 of the very best financial advisers whom they wanted to earn the opportunity to serve. Cody shared with Darren that they built a list of 1,000 financial advisers and then went to work to deliver more value than the other insurance marketing organizations in the industry to those 1,000.

The 1,000 advisers became their nation, and the advisers outside of their nation ceased to exist. Advisors Excel dedicated themselves to being the best they could be for this small group of prospects.

The outcome? Advisors Excel reached more than $4 billion in revenue by the end of year six in the business.

When they are the right prospects, you need only a small, passionate group of fans to make your business amazingly successful and profitable. Highly qualified prospects—whom you can support, and to whom you can add value—will be excited to do for you some of what you already did for them.

Ingredient #3: True Fans

Let's take the number 1,000 deeper, because it is a magical number and a vital priority in your business.

According to Kevin Kelly, if a business created a base of customers who were more like fans—1,000 true fans—then that business could become sustainable and profitable by simply focusing on the needs of its true fans.

The full text of Kevin Kelly's blog post as well as the long tail curve he created to illustrate the 1,000 true fans strategy can be found at http://kk.org/thetechnium/1000-true-fans/.

Kelly describes true fans as customers who will help you mobilize and move your business to that next level. They are true fans of you, true fans of your message, true fans of your business.

As I mentioned earlier in this chapter, they will support you because of the sacred bond you have built with them, a bond that was built upon—and continues to be built upon—the foundation of the value you consistently create and deliver.

Whether you do that every day or every week—no matter what the schedule, no matter what the rhythm—the fact that you are consistent is what is important.

According to Kevin, "A True Fan" is defined as someone who will purchase anything and everything you produce. True fans will drive 200 miles to visit your location. They will buy the super deluxe version of your product even though they already own the standard version.

They have a Google Alert set for your name. They have bookmarked your website.

They come to your product announcements or your ribbon-cutting ceremonies. They come to your book signings and ask for you to sign their copies.

They cannot wait for your next webinar, your next podcast episode, your next event, or your next release.

The best way to increase sales for your company is to connect with your True Fans directly. All you need is a podcast built on value. See? I keep coming back to that foundational truth.

A nation of 100 true fans is a reasonable number. As Kevin explains in his brilliant blog post: "If you added one fan a day, it would take only three years. True 'fanship' is doable. Pleasing a True Fan is pleasurable, and invigorating."

The key challenge is that you have to maintain direct contact with your 1,000 true fans. And you do that through building your platform—delivering value—and making sure you are using the right conduit so it reaches your 1,000 true fans on a consistent basis.

Again, it doesn't matter if you use a podcast, blog, robust LNKD profile and LNKD publishing, long-form posts on Medium, Instagram stories, Facebook Live, or any other format. What's important to identify isn't the platform on which you are most comfortable, but the platform your fans use the most. What is the best conduit to them?

For me, it's our *Onward Nation* podcast, my LinkedIn account, email campaigns, and webinars.

But there's another element to the recipe for building your nation of true fans. You will also build concentric circles of "lesser fans." Lesser fans might not seek out direct contact with you or your business, nor will they buy everything you produce. But they will buy *much* of what you produce.

The content, offerings, products, and processes you develop to feed your true fans will also nurture your lesser fans. As you build your nation of 1,000 true fans, you will also add many more lesser fans.

Lastly, as you are building, don't miss or avoid the opportunity to go deep—to develop intimacy with your audience. In fact, intimacy is one of the reasons why I ask for feedback in each of my *Onward Nation* "solocasts" (a solocast is an episode without a guest—just the host) and share my email address. My team and I legitimately want to get better, but I also want to hear from our audience and learn from them so that we can deliver even more value.

You now have a tangible recipe for building your own nation of true fans—and when you do, your nation will become this amazing, awesome, wonderful, beautiful, incredible community of people who are generous with their feedback and help guide your business in the right direction to deliver value.

Consider Kevin Kelly's lesson as you build your podcast. Ask yourself how you can continually add more and more value like Cody Foster and his team at Advisors Excel. Because when you build your nation, your business, your team, and your life will move onward to a completely new level.

✓ YOUR NATION-BUILDING CHECKLIST ✓

❑ Kick the impostor syndrome to the curb.

❑ Create and consistently deliver value, value, and more value through your platform—no way around this—value first.

❑ Ask for feedback, reply, and say thank you.

❑ Implement the recommendations you receive from your nation and publicly ask for more feedback.

❑ Your podcast guests are your nation so be sure to treat them like the VIPs they are.

CHAPTER 7

YOUR AVATAR, DREAM 50, AND MY $2 MILLION MISTAKE

The lessons in this chapter will help you solve one of the most expensive money-draining mistakes businesses make. The mistake occurs when there is ambiguity around identifying whom the business intends to serve as its customers. Business owners who think "everyone" is their prospect tend to spend more on marketing (often in the wrong media) and attend "networking" events that are not laser-focused.

Many business owners today are using expensive guesswork and trial and error. This chapter solves that problem.

You can eliminate the guesswork by getting a clear view of your ideal client and podcast listener. Not from a crystal ball but by asking yourself and your team the right questions. The outcome will be a clear view of your "client avatar"—an accurate representation of the people you want to attract to your podcast.

This chapter will remove the mystical dark magic voodoo to creating/defining your client avatar by giving you all the questions you need to answer. After defining your avatar, we will dig in and create your "Dream 50." Your Dream 50 prospect list represents the clients you would most like to serve in your industry. If you had the opportunity to serve them, it would be a game changer for your business.

In my experience, however, business owners tend to answer the question of "Who are your Dream 50?" with, "I would like to work with Harley Davidson, IBM, or our regional health-care provider network." But when business owners are asked to put pen to paper and write out the first name, last name, and title of the decision-maker at each of their Dream 50 businesses, their list-making momentum ends abruptly.

Who are they? Why do they matter to you? And once you know, what should you do with your Dream 50 list?

To help cement into place the importance of the Dream 50 lesson, I will share a painful $2 million mistake that I made, which could have ruined our business because I didn't pay attention to the lessons that were directly in front of me.

Apply the recipes in this chapter and you will remove the stress, pressure, and self-doubt you may be feeling about who you are intended to serve with your business.

When you don't define your avatar, when you don't define your Dream 50, and when you don't create a system for attracting those 50—what happens? You lose major amounts of opportunity in your business.

Here's the story of how I know this to be true.

Because of my ego and pride, I refused to listen to lessons Darren Hardy was trying to teach me during our monthly phone calls and in-person meetings.

I ignored my mentor's recommendations to precisely define our "Dream 50 Attendees"—the people we most wanted to attend our "Predictive ROI LIVE" event in January 2014, to connect this pool of VIPs back to the "avatar" of our ideal attendee, and then to craft a value proposition our avatar would care enough about to attend our live event.

I completed none of these.

It's not that Darren didn't tell, even urge me, to get this done. It's not that he didn't mentor me through the process. I had access to all of the help and support I needed, yet I still didn't take action.

I was paralyzed with fear. Plus, I was arrogant in thinking that prospective attendees would simply figure out our value proposition on their own.

Consequently, after selling a grand total of three seats for an event that had a $2 million operating budget, and shelling out $200,000 in expenses, we canceled Predictive ROI LIVE. Not awesome.

My hope is that you will learn from my mistakes—and how we fixed them—so you don't have to learn the same painful lesson.

Let's begin by looking at where we got off the path.

I was unwilling to face my fear and take the necessary time to answer three simple questions. Had I answered them, there would have been a completely different outcome.

Your answers to the three questions will guide your overall communication strategy with customers and prospects. Even deeper, your answers will establish your expertise and why your message is relevant and deserves to be heard.

But it is critically important that your answers come from the perspective of your client, not your ego. After all, those are vastly different perspectives.

I am also going to share with you a set of ten questions designed to help ensure that you are speaking to your avatar. Again, the ten questions are the same questions my team and I use at Predictive ROI to help our clients define their client avatar.

Had I taken the time to answer these questions—in precise detail—we likely would not have failed with our event. We would have either had a much more precisely defined value proposition or we would have discovered that, at that point in time, the scale of the event we were planning was way too large. We were swinging for the fences when we should have been paying closer attention to getting on base and scoring some runs.

Before we review the three questions to guide your overall communication strategy with customers and prospects, remember that your customers will not remember what you said, but how you made them *feel*.

In order for them to feel something as a result of what you said, you need to have established credibility in their mind's eye so you have permission to say what needs to be said.

Throughout the entire conversation—heck, you may even be doing it now as you read these words—your audience will ask themselves three simple questions, and you must answer them. Or the conversation is over.

- Question 1: Who are you?
- Question 2: Why do I care?
- Question 3: What's in it for me?

Now, you may not like the questions. They may be too direct for your particular communication style, but they are, in reality, the essence of what your customers are asking themselves as they listen to you.

The first two questions of "Who are you?" and "Why should I care?" are core credibility indicator questions. When beginning a conversation—especially with someone new—you need to answer these two questions as succinctly as possible.

The third question, "What's in it for me?" is the ultimate value proposition question. One of the reasons our Predictive ROI LIVE event failed was because I personally could never explain or define why a business owner would want to invest $7,000 and head to the Ritz-Carlton in Orlando, Florida, for four days to learn about digital marketing strategies.

The pricing was off, the value proposition was nonexistent, and the worst part was that Darren had asked me this same question during every call:

"Stephen, why would anyone want to come to this thing?"

I never set my ego aside. I never listened. I never answered his very simple question.

Once you have your core message defined, it's time to crystallize with whom you are going to share your message (your avatar!) and how to create an emotional impact with your audience by answering ten questions you and your team need to ask one another. No surface answers. Challenge yourself and your team. Dig deep and find specific examples of situations that reinforce or contradict what is currently believed to be true.

1. What are our customers' challenges right now?
2. What are our customers' emotional fears or worries?
3. What are their dreams and aspirations?
4. What are their pain points?
5. What are their values—and are they the same as ours?
6. Whom do they want to impress the most?
7. What frustrates them about our business or others like us in the industry?
8. What do they want from our business?
9. What's the one result that, if you could guarantee it, your customers would pay a premium for?
10. Finish this sentence on behalf of your customers as if they were saying this to you: "You will gain my trust and comfort by . . ."

Once you have collected that data, you will have all you need in order to create your avatar.

Some words of caution: Your avatar is one person. Not an email list of 25,000 people. Every piece of communication you send to your customers and prospect lists needs to speak directly to your avatar. And because of that you should give your avatar a name. Think of it as though you were having a one-on-one conversation with each email you send or social media post you create.

Hang a photo of your avatar on your conference room wall, and every time you write an email campaign or shoot a video, speak directly to it!

Let me take you inside Predictive ROI to illustrate this point. Our client avatars are named "Harry" and "Sally." We chose those names because *When Harry Met Sally* is one of my favorite movies of all time.

All of our conversations with Harry and Sally are personal—they are emotional—and they are always authentic.

This is Sally:

⬧ She and her team are ambitious and want to learn new things.
⬧ She knows there is more opportunity and growth "out there" and is frustrated she does not know how to capitalize on it, faster.

- She reads lots of books but doesn't know a good idea from a bad one.
- She is uncertain and afraid to fail.
- She has been fooled before and does not know whom to believe.
- She thinks everything sounds too good to be true.
- She has said to me, "Stephen, I want to trust that you can do what you say you can do. Show me the evidence quickly that it is working and that you are delivering on your promises."

During more than one presentation to a prospective client, "Sally" has said to me, "My goodness, that's me!" I love it when that happens because I know we just made a powerful, emotional connection.

Now what?

The final recipe in this lesson is another principle Darren taught me. He called it "Romancing Your Dream 50."

Your Dream 50 prospects fit two criteria: (1) They were aligned with your avatar so you are able to connect with them on an emotional level because you really understand them, and (2) They are the easiest to reach, they are the fastest to make a decision, they are the most profitable, and it would be your absolute dream to call these 50 *your* clients. The people who make it to your Dream 50 list likely represent your *best buyer* profile.

So how will you romance them? How will you show them how much they mean to you? How much value can you deliver to them—before you are working with or for them?

- Interview each of your Dream 50 on your podcast—and then quote and share their wisdom over social media and with your email list. Your email list will appreciate the additional insights, and your guest will think it's awesome how you spread the word. Great things will happen!
- Create an industry research report and ask your Dream 50 to participate in exchange for giving them a free copy of the report when the project is complete.

- Invite members of your Dream 50 to co-teach a webinar with you. This adds value to your list while giving you an exceptional opportunity to connect with your top prospects in a completely different way.

- Host a party, wine tasting, dinner, or similar event.

- Or, maybe you're a power connector with a titanium Rolodex. You effortlessly make connections. Awesome. Then solve the problems of your Dream 50 by introducing them to people who could help— people they would love to do business with. This adds tremendous value to your prospective clients. As a result, they may be open to doing business with you because of how you delivered and solved their needs first!

Those are just a few quick strategies for how you can "Romance Your Dream 50." I wish you the best in applying them and taking the definition of your avatar deeper than ever before.

✓ YOUR AVATAR CREATION CHECKLIST ✓

❑ Answer the questions of "Who are you?" "Why do I care?" and "What's in it for me?" on behalf of your audience because your answers will form the foundation of your podcast's value proposition.

❑ Complete the avatar exercise in this chapter.

❑ Give your avatar a name and introduce him or her to your team.

❑ Work with your team to define your Dream 50. Be specific with first names, last names, email addresses, and companies. "We're going to target the market leaders in the XYZ industry" is not sufficient.

❑ Describe how you will romance your Dream 50 and show them how much they mean to you.

❑ Review the plan with your team.

CHAPTER 8

STAGE 1:
STRATEGIC PLANNING AND PRODUCTION KICKOFF

Welcome to the seven stages of production for your profitable podcast. The next seven chapters provide all of the technical step-by-step recipes and ingredients you need to create and launch your podcast. Each stage contains several interdependent recipes all woven together into a cohesive production process.

Please trust the process—even if the order of a particular recipe seems out of place. For example, why would you begin website groundwork in Stage 2 when you haven't recorded any interviews yet? Rest assured, my team at Predictive ROI created this process from scratch, has made several comprehensive revisions to it, and has perfected it over hundreds of executions. Each recipe has been placed into the production process at the exact position to make the overall flow as smooth as possible. The launch of your podcast website will require several weeks of production time, so completing the groundwork early on in Stage 2 will help ensure that once your episodes are finished in post-production, they can be uploaded into Libsyn, and then immediately pulled into your website, which should be fully functional by then.

The beginning of each chapter includes a high-level illustration of that stage's major production milestones and overarching goal. In the case of Stage 1, your goal will be to complete the "Project Sheet" with all the details necessary to move on to Stage 2.

Let's move into Stage 1—Strategic Planning and Production Kickoff. Figure 8-1 illustrates the highlights of the production process in this stage.

The Project Sheet template (see Figure 8-2, pp. 80–82) is available for your free download at PredictiveROI.com/resources/Stage-1. It is a Google Sheets template so you can copy it into your Google Docs account and then share the file with all of the members of your team who are involved with the production of your podcast. The Project Sheet is designed to help you and your team keep all of the tasks in Stage 1 moving along efficiently.

You and your team should be able to accomplish all of the tasks with the Stage 1 Project Sheet during a ninety-minute kickoff.

FIGURE 8-1

This stage is all about covering the basic details we need to start production on your podcast.

EMAIL OUTLINING MATERIALS FOR MEETING 1

This email will be sent to you a week before our kickoff meeting. If it does not arrive, reach out to us or check your spam folder.

CONTACT INFO

This contact information will be used internally, externally, and in website and email designs.

DETAILS

There are a lot of moving parts and this will be a mixed bag of information such as the type of computer you use and the day of the week you want to have an episode go live.

GOALS, AUDIENCE & MONETIZATION

We will take a deep dive into the avatar of your listener and customers. Outline what success looks like for you. And define the real purpose of your podcast.

DECIDE ON NEXT MEETING

Pick a time within 7 to 9 days to do the next meeting and get it on everyone's calendar.

POST MEETING FOLLOW UP

Following the meeting you will get an email outlining what will need to be done before our next meeting.

Goal

Our goal during the meeting will be to complete a spreadsheet with all the details needed to move to Stage 2.

FIGURE 8-2

STAGE 1	Company Name–Name of Podcast		
	Job/Task	Status/Questions	Example Assets
	Recipe 1: Contact Information		
At Meeting	Address for billing		
At Meeting	Your time zone for settings		
At Meeting	Phone number to reach you		
At Meeting	Phone number for guests to reach you		
At Meeting	Phone number to put on website		
At Meeting	Email to reach you		
At Meeting	Email for guests to reach you		
At Meeting	Email to put on the website		
At Meeting	Email you want as a forwarding address from the email account listed above		
At Meeting	Email you want publicly on the podcast website		
At Meeting	Your Skype handle		
At Meeting	Legal business name for disclosures		
At Meeting	Email setup for sending out emails on your behalf: YourNamePodcast@Gmail.com		

FIGURE 8-2 (continued)

At Meeting	Email address YourNamePodcast@Gmail.com should forward to?
At Meeting	Email address YourNamePodcast@Gmail.com should look like?
Recipe 2: Details	
Via Email	Credit card info for third-party purchases
At Meeting	Do you use a Mac or PC?
At Meeting	Confirm how many epsiodes per week
At Meeting	Choose day of week for episodes to be posted
At Meeting	Determine how many podcasts need to be recorded and in the can before launch (4 for launch + 1 month of episodes. Minimum 10)
At Meeting	Which social media platforms are you currently using? LinkedIn, Twitter, Facebook.
At Meeting	Which social media platforms will you be posting podcast-related content to? Linkedin, Twitter, Facebook.
At Meeting	Will you be sending a guest alert email to let them know their "podcast is live"?
Recipe 3: Avatar, Monetization, Vital Priority, and Vital Metrics	
At Meeting	Kickoff Meeting: Discuss branding, topics for content (what do you want to learn?), and questions that will lead to research or content marketing assets.

FIGURE 8-2 (continued)

		Status/Questions	Example Assets
At Meeting	Review Dream 50 list		
At Meeting	Complete the avatar exercise		
STAGE 1	**Company Name–Name of Podcast**		
	Job/Task		
At Meeting	Choose podcast name		
At Meeting	Create podcast tagline (10 words or fewer)		
At Meeting	Decide on vital priority for podcast (grow revenue, expand platform, build nation of true fans, etc.)		
At Meeting	Identify three vital metrics that will be used to evaluate progress toward the vital priority (sales, email opt-ins, new social media connection, etc.)		
At Meeting	Vital metric 1:		
At Meeting	Vital metric 2:		
At Meeting	Vital metric 3:		
At Meeting	Who is your customer? Guest or audience?		
At Meeting	Create bookmarks in your web browser for Project Sheet, Airing Schedule, and social media folder.		
At Meeting	How would you describe your podcast to someone who knows nothing about it? Think elevator pitch for your podcast. X-Y-Z statement.		

Recipe 1: Contact Information

Contact Information on the Project Sheet will take you or someone on your team only a few minutes to fill out before your kickoff meeting.

Recipe 2: Details

Details continues with the tactical gathering of information into one location so you and your team won't have to continually search and hunt for the data points you will need on a consistent basis. The Google Sheet shown in Figure 8-3 (see next page) can be found as a template for free download at Predictive ROI.com/Resources/Stage-1 and will help you keep track of any third-party expenses associated with your podcast, whether they be monthly or onetime fees.

Recipe 3: Avatar, Monetization, Vital Priority, and Vital Metrics

This recipe involves several key strategic decisions that are important to make during the kickoff meeting because changing direction down the line will extend your timeline and potentially increase cost. For example, you and your team should also consider and answer the following questions:

- What topics do we want to use the podcast to help us learn more about so we can create content and thought leadership?
- What questions would help us collect the right information?
- Will the show be branded as its own platform, e.g., *Onward Nation* not *The Predictive ROI Podcast*? Or will your podcast and company brands be interchangeable?
- Next come decisions regarding interview type. What type of show format aligns best with our goals? Here are some questions to consider:
  - Are you the type of person who likes to keep conversations free flowing, open-ended, and spontaneous? If so, you may want to consider scripting out several questions for each guest in

FIGURE 8-3

Credit Card	Name on Card	Number	Expiration Date	CVV	Billing Address and Zip	Setup Complete?
Program	Link	Cost	Monthly or Onetime	Username	Password	
Schedule Once		$50.00	Monthly			
Libsyn		$20.00	Monthly			
Smart Podcast Player		$12.00	Monthly			
Stitcher		0				
iTunes		0				
Google Play		0				
Website hosting						
Website domain name		$40.00	Monthly			
Website security and support						
Hootsuite		$35.00	Monthly			
Professional recorded intro/outro		$350 to $600	Onetime			
Add-ons						
Photos for e-books		$40.00	Monthly			

advance by doing your research but letting your guest know you plan to "go off script" and head down paths that come up during discussion.

- Or, you may want to follow a specific interview flow with predetermined questions you can email to your guests in advance for their review. The majority of *Onward Nation* guests appreciate having an opportunity to review the questions as well as prepare their answers in advance of the interview. The rare exceptions are guests like author Gary Vaynerchuk or marketing expert Chris Brogan who prefer to be 100 percent spontaneous in their answers during the interview. That is not a good fit for the majority of guests. We recommend you prepare a specific list of questions, save it as a PDF, and provide it to your guests in the invitation as well as one of the interview reminders. We will cover the details of this process during Stage 2.

- Do you want to use your podcast purely as a "solocast"? This is ideal for thought leadership–focused podcasts where the host is the star. But, this format will limit your opportunity to use your podcast to grow revenue because, as we discussed in Chapter 4, your Dream 50 prospect list would not make their way onto your show. Or, perhaps you and your team would prefer a hybrid method where you offer your audience an occasional solocast for thought leadership but the majority of your episodes will consist of interviews with your Dream 50 prospects as your guests. Regardless of your preference, the kickoff meeting is the time to make your decision regarding show format.

- "Avatar" is listed as an ingredient in Recipe 3. However, if you've been working through this book in a linear process, you will have already completed your Avatar exercise back in Chapter 7.

- What will you name your podcast? Is there a domain name available for the podcast name you like the most?

- We recommend the title of your show be something independent of your company and sync up well with the interests of your Dream 50. For example, our client avatar at Predictive ROI (Sally) is ambitious, and she wants to learn new things and is looking for practical and tactical strategies for moving her business onward to that next level. Because we know this about Sally, we decided to name our podcast *Onward Nation* and give it the tagline, "Learn how to think, act, & achieve like today's top business owners." Develop a name for your show that your Dream 50 will be drawn toward.
- You also ought to consider filing for a federal trademark to protect your show name. The last thing you want is to build a popular podcast only to find out the hard way that you infringed on an existing trademark in the process.
- Once you know the trademark is clear, register the domain name for your podcast.

▸ Next you will need to define the "vital priority" and "vital metrics" of your podcast. Both of these topics were covered in depth in Chapter 2; now you'll need to enter them into your Project Sheet.

▸ The final ingredient—being able to describe your podcast to someone who is not familiar with it—is important because your approach to this will be used as the foundation for your intro and outro scripts in Chapter 10: Stage 3.

✓ YOUR STRATEGIC PLANNING CHECKLIST ✓

❑ Schedule a ninety-minute kickoff session with you and your team.

❑ Be prepared to lead a discussion around the content and thought leadership the podcast should create in order to align with the vital priorities you defined earlier.

❑ Work with your team to define the vital metrics for the podcast. How will success be defined and measured?

❑ Enter all of the data into your Project Sheet and share it with your team.

CHAPTER 9

STAGE 2:
GUEST EXPERIENCE
AND WEBSITE GROUNDWORK

Welcome to Stage 2 of production for your profitable podcast. Your overarching goal for completing Stage 2 is to put a system into place that ensures that your guests have a good experience leading up to their interview. We call this the Guest Advocacy System. It's a strategic process that cares for your guests between when they register for an interview on your show and when the interview takes place. The Guest Advocacy System will help your guests prepare for their interviews.

The strategy consists of an easy-to-use online registration system, automated thank-you and reminder emails that feel personal, reminders via text message, a question list, an equipment list to make sure guests sound as great as possible, and a marketing guide guests can use to help them get maximum exposure from their interview. In total, the Guest Advocacy System consists of numerous communications designed to make guests feel well cared for and to help build anticipation for the interview.

This chapter also includes instructions for how to set up the scheduling software and email templates, as well as examples of checklists so you can have a top-notch Guest Advocacy System at the ready.

In addition, Stage 2 will guide you through the process of collecting the initial website groundwork so your team can begin building a site that will serve as your podcast's digital headquarters.

Lastly, all emails, Question Flows, and other templates are available in their native file formats for you to download for free at PredictiveROI.com/Resources/Stage-2.

Now, let's move into Stage 2. Figure 9-1 highlights this stage's production process.

The Project Sheet template in Figure 9-2 (see pp. 92–93) is available for your free download at PredictiveROI.com/resources/Stage-2. As with documents in Stage 1, it, too, is a Google Sheet template so you can copy it into your Google Docs account and then share the file with all of the members of your team who are involved with the production of your podcast. The Project Sheet is designed to help you and your team keep all of the tasks within Stage 2 moving along efficiently. There are many moving parts in Stage 2 so the Project Sheet is a valuable asset for keeping the process organized.

You and your team will likely need one to two weeks to complete Stage 2.

FIGURE 9-1

2

This stage is all about covering the communications and guest experience when registering a guest with you.

EMAIL OUTLINING MATERIALS FOR MEETING #2

This email will be sent to you before our next meeting. It outlines the documents we need you to review and approve.

EMAILS & DISCLOSURES

These emails and disclosures will be sent via ScheduleOnce to guests.

QUESTIONS

This will be a first draft of your questions. These are not set in stone, but they are a place to get started.

GUEST PREP GUIDE

We want to make sure your guests are as prepared as possible for the interview. This document will help with that. But keep in mind, ultimately, you are their guide and the gatekeeper on audio quality.

DECIDE ON NEXT MEETING

Pick a time within 7 to 9 days to do the next meeting and get it on everyone's calendar.

POST MEETING FOLLOW-UP

Following the meeting you will get an email outlining what will need to be done before our next meeting.

Goal

Our goal during the meeting will be to make sure your guests have a good experience before the interview and feel prepared.

FIGURE 9-2

STAGE 2	Company Name–Name of Podcast	
	Job/Task	**Status/Questions**
	Recipe 1: Initial Documents	
Email	Prepare first draft of Question Flow	
Email	Write guest confirmation email	
Email	Write guest reminder email	
Email	Create "Sound Brilliant" Guide	
Email	Create your legal disclosure	
Email	Decide ScheduleOnce fields needed for guest registration	
	Recipe 2: ScheduleOnce Setup	
Meeting	Gmail account associated with calendar is connected	
Meeting	Build custom form fields based on selections in Recipe 1	
Meeting	Put guest confirmation email from Recipe 1 into place	
Meeting	Put guest reminder emails from Recipe 1 into place	
Meeting	Add legal disclosure from Recipe 1 to end of confir-mation emails	
Meeting	Select and install headshot photo of host	
Meeting	Decide SMS package to purchase. This is for text alerts to you and/or your guests.	
Meeting	Reminder texts built	
Meeting	Attach final version of Question Flow and Sound Brilliant Guide to confirmation emails	
Meeting	Send registration link to host	
Meeting	Decide who on the team is in charge of the host's calendar	
Meeting	Select interview availability: time slots made available for interviewing guests	

STAGE 2	Company Name–Name of Podcast	
	Job/Task	**Status/Questions**
	Recipe 3: Website Groundwork	
Meeting	Need to determine URL for website	
Meeting	Hosting company selected	
Meeting	Name of hosting company	
Meeting	Username	
Meeting	Password	
Meeting	Domain name purchased	
Meeting	Name of domain company	
Meeting	Username	
Meeting	Password	
Meeting	Who will do maintenance?	

Recipe 1: Initial Documents

This is where you will create the majority of assets necessary to complete Stage 2. For example, you and your team will create your Question Flow for guests as well as a series of confirmation emails and a sound guide; you'll also make some decisions regarding a third-party scheduling software that will enable you to automate much of your Guest Advocacy System.

In my opinion, a top-notch Guest Advocacy System includes an online scheduling system, calendar integration, and the creation of interview reminders and equipment recommendations for guests. It not only provides your guests with what they need in order to be great on your show, but also provides you as the host with the critical information you need in order to facilitate an excellent interview.

All of the sample emails in this chapter are available as templates that you can download for free at PredictiveROI.com/resources/Stage-2.

Let's begin with your *Question Flow*, which is your list of questions in the order you plan to ask them during your interviews with guests. This is not a random set of discussion points or poorly crafted, amateur questions that are interesting only on the surface. You need to be strategic. Every question matters when putting your best foot forward with your guests.

Your questions must be top shelf so that when prospective guests review them as they consider whether to accept or reject your invitation, they will be impressed by your business acumen. Write questions that are not typical and organize them into a flow that makes logical sense.

Begin by asking a couple of "break the ice" questions. Then after some rapport has been built, you can take the discussion deeper with your third question. Ultimately, your questions need to sync up with the topics you want to learn more about and the knowledge you want to pass on to your audience. The answers your guests provide should help you better understand their businesses so you can evaluate if there could be an opportunity between your two companies in the future.

Figure 9-3 and Figure 9-4 are examples of the two Question Flows we use at *Onward Nation*. Figure 9-3 shows the standard set of questions that we have used for the majority of our episodes. However, there have been a number of guests whom we have invited back to the show for a special encore interview. In those instances, we want to ask them a completely different set of questions (Figure 9-4). But the encore questions build on the momentum created during their first interview.

I encourage you to follow a similar process. Your guests and your audience will appreciate your attention to detail.

Recipe 1 continues with the creation of several confirmation emails each of your Dream 50 prospects will receive once they complete the registration process to appear as a guest on your show. We recommend using ScheduleOnce as your scheduling software and as your primary distribution point for the confirmation emails.

We selected ScheduleOnce for the system because of its ease of integration with Gmail, Google Calendar, and Infusionsoft (our preferred CRM). We have found ScheduleOnce to be easy to work with, offer great support, and straightforward to install and set up.

FIGURE 9-3

Introduction

1) I will give a brief introduction of you and your business and then turn it over to you to share more.

Focus and Preparation

2) Is there a secret, timesaving technique you can share with Onward Nation that helps you focus and tackle your most vital priorities each day?

3) What is one of your daily habits you strongly believe contributes to your success?

Overcoming Obstacles

4) Tell us about a challenging time or situation that could have devastated or even ruined your business but, you persisted -- you made the tough decisions. And now, that once painful memory, serves as an invaluable learning experience.

Personal Mastery

5) What is the most critical skill you think business owners need to master in order to thrive today?

Lessons Learned

6) Tell us about the most influential lesson you ever learned from one of your mentors and how it helped you become the business owner you are today.

Breaking Down the Recipe for Success

We all know that building and scaling a business is hard work. But when we have the right strategy -- that right "recipe" to follow -- then the action steps become more like "ingredients" and can be added systematically into the business -- one ingredient at a time.

The end result is a business that is systematic, predictable, and repeatable. The business owner, along with his or her business, can produce the same result for customers time and time again.

In this final round of our interview -- I will ask you to break down your "recipe" of success and the "ingredients" that helped along your path.

7) If there was a magic "reset" button as it relates to starting your business...what systems would you go back and put into place sooner rather than later...and why?

8) What one strategy -- or recipe -- that if business owners and their teams could consistently apply every day -- would compound into big wins for them?

9) Fast-forward one year. You're looking back on the hiring decisions you are considering making now. And imagine the people you hired today exceeded your highest expectations. What recipe or strategy did they consistently apply that delivered the most value to your business?

10) Imagine you are standing in front of a room business owners -- people -- just like you when you were starting out. They are battling their way through the fears, worries, doubts, and struggles to find their footing. What are two or three strategies you would recommend they focus on to best ensure success?

Please note: I will call you via Skype at the appointed time. Skype: stephen.woessner. This is an audio only interview.

Interview Flow Sample   www.onwardnation.com

FIGURE 9-4

ONWARDNATION

Encore Interview Flow Sample

Introduction

1) I know you have been working on some exciting projects as you prepare for the next 12-months — so — bring us up to speed on what's new and what has you excited for the road ahead.

Focus and Preparation

2) Please start off this ENCORE discussion by taking us behind the scenes...and into your process...your recipe...your daily routine for how do you begin the first 60-minutes of your day.

3) Do you have a favorite quote or lesson you can share with us that helps you keep a focused mindset throughout the day?

Defining Success

4) Each person's definition of success can and should be different. But success can also be a difficult or intangible thing for a business owner to define so having models or examples to consider can make it easier. So please be our mentor here, and share how you define success.

Personal Mastery

5) Les Brown once said that "Most people don't work on their dreams because of fear. The fear of failure, 'what if things don't work out'? And then the fear of success, 'what if they do and I can't handle it'? Fear — in all its shapes and sizes is something that we as business owners — deal with. So...do you have a couple of strategies or tips you use to help push aside those stubborn roadblocks, the challenges, the doubts, the fears, that can sometimes rise up and try to impede this journey you are on?

Hiring "A Players"

6) We as business owners often hear that we need to hire "A players" as members of our organization. In your opinion...what makes an "A player" an "A player"?

Breaking Down the Recipe for Success

7) During our first conversation, we talked about the most influential lesson you ever learned from one of your mentors and how that lesson helped you become the business owner you are today. Now let's take the mentorship topic deeper and focus our attention on how we as business owners can become better mentors. What would be two or three strategies you would recommend for improving how we mentor those around us every day?

8) I oftentimes hear experts say things like, "today's business owners need to build a platform — they need to build an audience — build a tribe — build a community." I even catch myself saying it from time-to-time. So, if building a platform is truly a vital priority, what would be two or three strategies you would recommend that business owners consistently apply in order to make that happen?

9) Imagine you are standing in front of a room of business owners who are all striving to get to that proverbial "next level" with their company. These owners are beyond the startup — they have successfully battled their way through the initial fears and built solid momentum. What would be two or three strategies you would recommend they focus on to help them move off their current plateau and leap onward to that next level?

Please note: I will call you via Skype at the appointed time. Skype: stephen.woessner. This is an audio only interview.

Encore Interview Flow Sample   www.onwardnation.com

You and your team should also take the opportunity to integrate Schedule-Once with a Gmail and Google account for the host so that when interviews are booked, they are dynamically added to the host's calendar.

We interact with each of our *Onward Nation* guests as many as ten times before and immediately following the interview:

- *Touch 1*: personalized guest invitation from me including interview Question Flow sample attached. I will provide you with a template of the invitation in one of the upcoming stages.
- *Touch 2*: booking confirmation email sent via ScheduleOnce with interview questions attached for a second time. The guest received the questions the first time via my initial invitation (see Figure 9-5).

FIGURE 9-5

Title of email should be: Booking Confirmation V1.

Everything in brackets and bolded is a variable that needs to be changed manually by you or your team.

Font sizes for paragraph text is size 12.

Everything in brackets not bolded is a system dynamic field.

Delete interviewer headshot space from email template.

The guest headshot is an attachment type field in the form build.

Subject: Your interview time with **[Name of interviewer or podcast]** is set!

Your interview booking is confirmed.

Dear **[Customer name]**,

Your interview booking is confirmed. Please see below for more information. DOUBLE CHECK TO MAKE SURE YOUR CALENDAR'S TIME ZONE IS ACCURATE.

Here is the [list of questions] I will be asking you.

In addition, [here is a guide] to make sure we make the most out of our time and make sure you sound great!

Booking details:

Time:
[Starting date and time in customer's time zone]

Calendar event:

If the event is not already in your calendar, you may add it from here:
[Calendar images and links]

Your information:
Your name: [customer name]
Your company: [customer company]
Your mobile phone number: [customer phone]

◆ *Touch 3*: booking confirmation email sent to guests along with interview questions and "Sound Brilliant" recommendations. Please note: We attach the questions on multiple occasions because when we did it only twice early on some guests commented that they didn't receive the questions. However, once we moved to three distributions we have not received another complaint (see Figure 9-6).

FIGURE 9-6

Your booking is confirmed

Dear Stephen Woessner,

Your booking is confirmed. Please see below for more information. DOUBLE-CHECK TO MAKE SURE YOUR CALENDAR'S TIME ZONE IS ACCURATE.

Here is the list of questions I will be asking you.

In addition, here is a great document detailing how to make your interview sound amazing!

Booking details

Time:
Thu, Jan 7, 2016, 01:00pm–02:00pm
United States; Central time (GMT-6)
Cancel/Reschedule

Calendar event

If the event is not already in your calendar, you may add it from here:

| Add to Outlook Calendar | Add to Google Calendar | Add to Calendar | Add to other Calendars |

Your information

Your name:
Stephen Woessner

Company:
Predictive ROI

Your mobile phone:

+1 (608) 498-5165

Please note: By participating in the Business Rescue Roadmap interview, you agree to allow Stacy Tuschl, LLC to record, distribute, and disseminate the podcast in any manner. You also agree to allow Stacy Tuschl, LLC to retain rights to the produced media for potential future use in speeches, books, and in all other public distribution.

♦ *Touch 4*: twenty-four-hour reminder email sent via Infusionsoft (or whatever email distribution/CRM system you decide to use). We integrated ScheduleOnce with our Infusionsoft account, which pulls all of our guest information into our CRM system so we can easily send future follow-ups and promotional campaigns to our guests—and only our guests (see Figure 9-7). Please note: ScheduleOnce integrates with several other platforms. Infusionsoft is not a prerequisite to being successful in using ScheduleOnce.

FIGURE 9-7

Title of email(s) should be: Customer Notification One Week V1, Customer Notification One Day. V1, Customer Notification One Hour V1.

Everything in brackets and bolded is a variable that needs to be changed manually.

Font sizes for paragraph text is size 12.

Everything in brackets not bolded is a system dynamic field.

Delete interviewer headshot from email template.

The guest headshot is an attachment type field in the form build.

Subject: Your interview with **[Name of interviewer or podcast]** starts at [Time and date]

Your interview is starting at [Time and date]

Dear [Customer name],

Your interview is starting in just **[x number of days or hours]** at [Starting date and time in customer's time zone]. It is going to be AWESOME! Please see below for more information. Any questions you have, feel free to reach out to [interviewer email].

In case you need a reminder of the questions, <u>you can go here</u>.

Also, if you didn't have a chance to look before, **here is a guide** to help make sure your interview goes smoothly and sounds great.

Booking details:
. . . .

[Starting date and time in customer's time zone]

Calendar event:
. . . .

If the event is not already in your calendar, you may add it from here: [Calendar images and links]

Your information:
Your name: [customer name]
Company: [customer company]
Your mobile phone: [customer mobile phone]

Please note: By participating in the [Podcast Name] interview, you agree to allow [Legal name of entity] to record, distribute, and disseminate the podcast in any manner. You also agree to allow [Legal name of entity] to retain rights to the produced media for potential future use in speeches, books, and in all other public distribution.

- *Touch 5*: forty-eight-hour reminder text. Guests have told us they value the interview reminders we send via text in addition to the email reminders. We have had only one guest miss an interview due to forgetting.
- *Touch 6*: twenty-four-hour reminder text.
- *Touch 7*: sixty-minute reminder text.
- *Touch 8*: Send a "Thank You" email immediately following the interview.
- *Touch 9*: Send a "Preview Links" twenty-four hours before the guest's interview airs.
- *Touch 10*: Send a "You're Live on [Insert Your Show Name]!" the morning a guest's show airs along with the link on your website where they can find their show.

We developed the following "Sound Brilliant" Guide as a way to help guests get prepared for the interview from a technical perspective. You will want your guests to sound as crystal clear as possible. The quality of their audio affects your listeners' willingness to continue listening to your episode. If your guest has a bad headset, no headset, noise in the background, or any of the myriad of other noisy distractions that can occur, your listeners will move on to another podcast.

Sound Brilliant!

Thanks again for agreeing to be a guest on my podcast, [insert name of your podcast here]. I want you to sound as brilliant as I know you are. Part of that's on me as your interviewer. But part of it is as simple as having the right equipment to record the conversation.

I want you and your brand to be represented in the best possible light, so please read through the list below and make any of the suggested adjustments you are able to make prior to our conversation. Following these suggestions will enable us to make the most of our time.

The Environment

NOTE! If it is a bad audio recording we can do only so much in post-production editing! Remember, garbage in, garbage out. So please make sure you review this so my team and I can make you sound great.

Turn off all nonessential programs on your computer to enable our recording to happen with less potential for technical glitches or unplanned pings or chimes.

Find a quiet place for our conversation.

Make sure all potential noisemakers are turned off or taken care of ahead of time (phones, email, kids, pets, etc.).

While we're doing our interview, please don't bump the table, scoot things around your desk, click pens, or anything else that might make noise. It's amazing what the mic can pick up.

Have a glass of water nearby during our chat . . . you may need it.

The Equipment

The microphone and speakers that are built in on your computer won't provide the sound quality we need. They'll mess with your volume/tone, and we'll get feedback. So please don't use them.

Even a microphone that is built in to your earbuds is better than your computer microphone.

I'm not suggesting that you need to buy a microphone or headset. But if you do a fair amount of these kinds of interviews, you may want to consider it. If not, ask around. You probably know someone who owns this sort of equipment and would lend it to you.

Make sure your computer speakers are turned completely down and you've set your computer's preferences to know that you're going to hear sound through headphones or earbuds instead. This will help us avoid feedback and electronic echo in the recording.

I know it's the twenty-first century, but if you can, please use a wired computer connection (not wireless) if at all possible.

Thanks again for agreeing to chat with me. I can't wait to connect my audience to you and your smarts. I promise I will do my best to make you sound brilliant!

[Your Name]
[Your Company]
[Youremail@youremail.com]

Each of the emails you send via your Guest Advocacy System should include a legal disclaimer. You want to ensure that you have clearly stated, multiple times, that you are free to use and distribute the content from the recorded episodes.

Recipe 2: ScheduleOnce Account Setup

It is time to complete your ScheduleOnce account setup so you can pull in the content you created as part of Recipe 1. The outcome of these simple steps will be a confirmation email.

As a host, I find it helpful to have all of a guest's contact information at my fingertips (see Figure 9-8). On multiple occasions, due to a simple mix-up, I have attempted to connect with our guest via Skype and the person didn't pick up. But the guest did answer a cell phone. You can't be nimble on your feet like that if you don't have the mobile numbers handy. In addition, if you don't have guests' mobile numbers, you won't be able to use ScheduleOnce to send SMS text reminders of your interview.

FIGURE 9-8

Your Dream 50 prospects should go through a formal registration process to get "booked" for an appearance as a guest on your show.

Below is a list of fields we typically ask guests to complete. These fields are guidelines. Please feel free to modify them based on the data points you would like to collect from each of your Dream 50 prospects.

We recommend that you do keep the fields marked as **Mandatory**. These fields will be helpful to you during the interview and to your team as they produce the Show Notes for each episode.

- Your name **Mandatory**
- Your email **Mandatory**
- Your mobile phone **Mandatory**
- Your title
- Your company

- Your website URL
- Your Twitter handle (This helps us promote your episode to our social media community)
- Your Skype handle (This helps us connect on Skype for the interview) **Mandatory**
- Your public/business/personal Facebook page link (This lets us add a link to your Facebook page when we promote your episode on Facebook for increased downloads)
- Your mailing address
- Would you like something promoted in the Show Notes (e.g., product launch, book release, upcoming speech, etc.)? **Mandatory**
- Your bio/story (This is used for the website and during the podcast intro) **Mandatory**
- Your headshot (This is for the website) **Mandatory**

Providing your Dream 50 list with a properly organized and structured reservation system also creates an excellent first impression with the business leaders who also represent your prospective clients. If your Guest Advocacy System is top notch, you will leave an excellent impression. If it's lackluster, what does that tell your Dream 50 about what it may be like to work with you and your team?

Finishing your ScheduleOnce setup requires you to select which fields are mandatory during the registration process. Figure 9-9 illustrates how we have our *Onward Nation* account configured as well as how we configure the Schedule-Once accounts for the majority of our clients. Following the same process will save you some valuable setup time.

FIGURE 9-9

Below are the final details for completing the setup for your ScheduleOnce account.

In addition, here is a rundown of what you will be doing at this step in the recipe:

1. You or your team will be setting up a piece of software called Schedule-Once. If you already have this software, you can use your existing account.

2. What is the email you want your team to have people reach out to if they have questions during or after the registration?

3. What is one other email address (aside from what you listed above) that you would like alerted if someone registers, cancels, or reschedules?

4. What is the phone number you want registrants to be able to reach you at?

5. Your team will need a headshot of you to use in the scheduling software and on the website.

Your headshot will be used in several places:

#1: Within your scheduling software
#2: On your "About" page on the website
#3: If you do any solocasts (episodes without a guest)

Your headshot should be current and something you are comfortable with. It can show your personality as well!

The size just has to be smaller than 3MB.

The picture can be either square or portrait but not landscape.

6. Who on your team is going to be involved in your scheduling software and managing your calendar?

Recipe 2 is also where you need to decide if you will use the SMS text option available in ScheduleOnce to send the reminders outlined earlier in Touch 5, 6, and 7 of Recipe 1. In addition, you will need to complete and pull in final versions of your Question Flow and Sound Brilliant Guide and link them to your guest confirmation emails.

The final ingredient for finishing your ScheduleOnce setup is managing your availability to conduct interviews. You will include your general registration link to your interview calendar (managed via ScheduleOnce) within your invitation to your prospective guests. They will click on the link and attempt to find a day/time on your interview schedule that is convenient for them. But you will want to preset your inventory so you specify how many interviews you are open to recording each week—and on what days and during which time slots. For example, some of our clients open up four to five interview slots on the first Tuesday of the month, record all four interviews on that one day, and then they are done with recording for the entire month. For *Onward Nation*, I record interviews only on Tuesdays, and because we air a daily show, there are times where I may have eight interviews scheduled on a Tuesday. But in one day, I have recorded nearly two weeks of airing inventory.

Managing your availability within ScheduleOnce is easy. But to ensure that the scheduling, rescheduling, canceling, etc., process is as efficient as possible, you and your team need to integrate ScheduleOnce with your Google calendar so that reservations are automatically added and removed from your calendar by guests without any intervention on your part, assuming you have managed your inventory properly.

You can manage your availability within ScheduleOnce using the following steps:

1. Log into your ScheduleOnce account.
2. Once logged in, click on the "Configuration" link in the upper left navigation menu.
3. You will then be presented with a long vertical list of options in the center of your screen. Click on the option entitled "Availability."

4. This will take you to the week-by-week calendar. When you drag your mouse over a time slot, ScheduleOnce will highlight the time slot in green. You can highlight time slots in thirty-minute increments. You can highlight as many time slots as you like. And then in the lower left of the calendar screen you will see a forward and backward arrow. You can move one week forward or one week backward by clicking the respective arrows.

5. Be sure to click the orange "Save" button before leaving Schedule-Once, otherwise all of the inventory changes you made will be lost.

Now that you're finished with your inventory availability, when prospective guests visit your scheduling link, they will see a screen similar to what is shown in Figure 9-10.

FIGURE 9-10

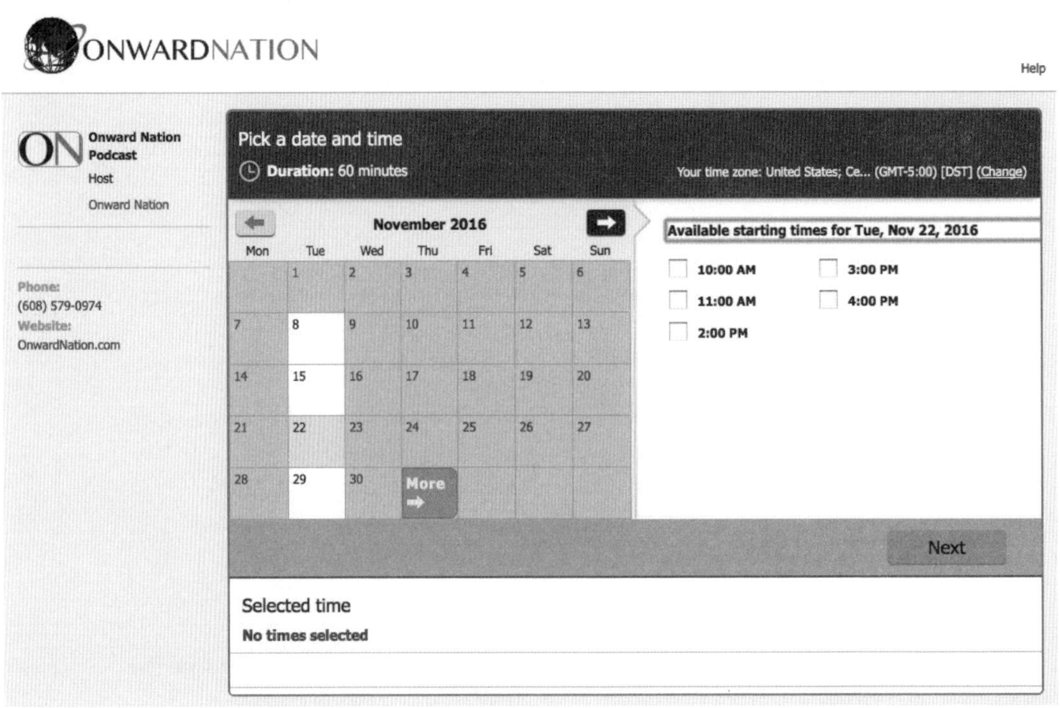

Recipe 3: Website Groundwork

Stage 2 concludes with you and your team thinking through several groundwork discussion points regarding what will eventually become the website for your podcast. Your podcast website will essentially be the digital headquarters for your show. It will house all of your episodes, any content marketing assets leveraged from your audio (Chapter 4), and your contact information.

You and your team should consider creating your podcast website using WordPress because of the podcast-friendly plug-ins you will be able to access. For example, the Smart Podcast Player is the leading player in the industry, user-friendly, and professional. At present, the player works only in WordPress.

✓ WEBSITE GROUNDWORK CHECKLIST ✓

As you complete your groundwork, I recommend that you take some time to consider the following:

❑ Decide on a website URL (you may have already completed this during Stage 1).

❑ Decide who you will use as a hosting company—it could be your existing hosting company

❑ Purchase the domain name.

❑ Decide who on your team will serve as the point person for maintenance regarding the website and the hosting account, that is, WordPress updates, security, plug-in updates, etc.

Time to move onward to Stage 3!

CHAPTER 10

STAGE 3:
AUDIO INTROS, OUTROS, AND DESIGN

Welcome to Stage 3 of production for your profitable podcast. Your overarching goal for completing this stage is to make sure you are prepared to conduct great interviews and capture listeners with a polished podcast feel.

Stage 3 is where the auditory and visual elements of your podcast will come to life. You and your team will be able to follow our recipes for how to write your intro and outro scripts along with completing the final prep work so you are ready to begin recording interviews with your guests. We have included our Interview Prep Guide to share insights and processes we have collected after having conducted, or produced, nearly 1,000 episodes across the Onward Nation Network over the past twenty-four months.

We also included our design guidelines and specifications you will need to create the visual representation for your podcast on your website and in iTunes, social media, or any other public touch point.

Lastly, this chapter also includes a framework for helping you select your podcast's format while giving you several things to consider as you think about which iTunes categories will be the most relevant for your show.

As in the previous chapters, I encourage you to visit PredictiveROI.com/resources/Stage-3 for a variety of downloadable resources, guides, and templates.

Figure 10-1 illustrates the highlights of the production process in this stage.

FIGURE 10-1

3

This stage is all about setting the stage for your podcast interviews and how you want to present your podcast to the world.

EMAIL OUTLINING MATERIALS FOR STAGE 3
This email will be sent to you before our next meeting. It outlines the documents we need you to review and approve.

INTROS & OUTROS
These audio clips are what start and close every episode. They need to tell the world quickly and passionately what your podcast is about and how listeners can stay connected to you.

PODCAST STRUCTURE & DESIGN
We will cover exactly how you want your podcast to be structured and how it looks so it helps achieve your goals.

PREPARING FOR AN INTERVIEW
We talked about preparing your guests, now let's talk about preparing you for the interview.

DECIDE ON NEXT MEETING
Pick a time within 7 to 9 days to do the next meeting and get it on everyone's calendar.

POST MEETING FOLLOW-UP
Following the meeting you will get an email outlining what will need to be done before our next meeting.

Goal
Our goal during the meeting will be to make sure you are prepared to do great interviews and capture listeners with a polished podcast feel.

The Stage 3 Project Sheet (Figure 10-2) template is available for your free download at PredictiveROI.com/resources/Stage-3. As with the Stages 1 and 2 Project Sheets, it's a Google Sheet template so you can copy it into your Google Docs account and then share the file with all of the members of your team who are involved in the production of your podcast.

FIGURE 10-2

STAGE 3	Company Name–Name of Podcast	
	Job/Task	Status/Questions
	Recipe 1: Design	
Meeting	Designate a designer/contact person as the go-to person for image assets, logos, headshots, etc.	
Meeting	Do you have anything special about your logo or name? Fonts, images, etc.?	
Meeting	Any color schemes, style guides, slogans, or other items that would be helpful when creating the website and logos?	
Meeting	What is the font style you want if you have a preference? Example: the same font as your current website, etc.	
Meeting	What are the color codes you have on your website and/or want to reuse?	
	Recipe 2: Assets to Create/Review	
Meeting	Create intro/outro scripts	
Meeting	Review intro/outro questions	
Meeting	Review and select episode structure	
Meeting	Review Interview Prep Guide	
Meeting	Review and select iTunes categories	

You and your team will likely need a week or two to complete Stage 3.

Recipe 1: Show Artwork and Digital Design Assets

You will need to create several digital assets that play various roles in the distribution of your show. The Digital Design Asset Guide in this chapter (Figures 10-3 and 10-4) includes all of the design specifications you and your team will need to consider when designing each asset.

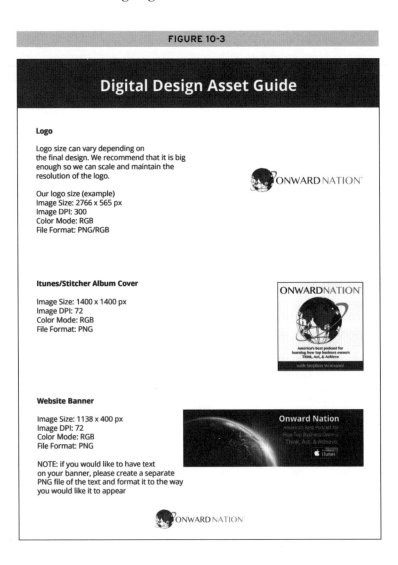

FIGURE 10-3

Digital Design Asset Guide

Logo

Logo size can vary depending on the final design. We recommend that it is big enough so we can scale and maintain the resolution of the logo.

Our logo size (example)
Image Size: 2766 x 565 px
Image DPI: 300
Color Mode: RGB
File Format: PNG/RGB

Itunes/Stitcher Album Cover

Image Size: 1400 x 1400 px
Image DPI: 72
Color Mode: RGB
File Format: PNG

Website Banner

Image Size: 1138 x 400 px
Image DPI: 72
Color Mode: RGB
File Format: PNG

NOTE: if you would like to have text on your banner, please create a separate PNG file of the text and format it to the way you would like it to appear

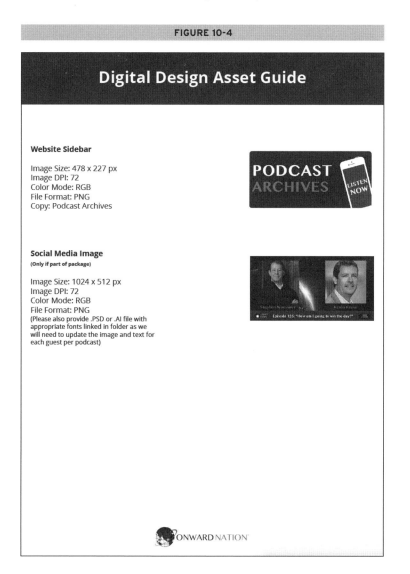

First, you'll need to design a logo for your podcast. The logo will be used on your website as well as on any other collateral materials you decide to produce to promote your show.

Second, create your show artwork. This will be your podcast's logo in iTunes, on your podcast player, and on your listeners' devices. Three key elements of your show artwork are your show name, tagline, and host name.

Third, depending on your podcast's website design, you will likely need to create some sort of banner that contains your show's tagline. Also consider including the iTunes and Stitcher logos as visual credibility indicators within the banner.

Fourth, consider creating a series of website sidebar graphics to promote your archives, special downloads to build your email list, rate and review requests, etc. Again, OnwardNation.com will provide you with visual examples to follow.

You and your team will be ready to move on to producing your podcast's website once you have all of the visual assets complete.

Recipe 2: Audio Assets to Create and Review

I recommend that you have a professional intro and outro produced for your podcast if you want your show to be a legitimate source of leads and revenue for your business. Value and brevity are the keys to creating a quality intro and outro. Your audience may feel as they were thrown into the episode if your intro is too short. Or, they may begin to get impatient if your intro runs for sixty seconds without providing any substance. It has been our experience that intros and outros of twenty to thirty seconds tend to be ideal.

The following questions will help you think through the basics—and a few specifics—for your intro and outro scripts.

The Basics

1. What is the name of your show?
2. What is the format of your show (e.g., interview vs. solo or co-hosted)?
3. What is the general category of your show (e.g., business, comedy, news, religion)?
4. Who is your target audience (e.g., your listener "avatar")?
5. What is the tone and vibe of your show (e.g., educational and reserved vs. rockin' and irreverent)?

6. How long have you been in this field? What is your background in this subject area?
7. What made you decide to go down the path of education/podcasting?

About Your Introduction

1. Do you have examples of other podcast introductions that you like? Dislike?
2. Do you have any specific taglines or dialogue you want to use in your intro (e.g., "join the tribe")?
3. How do you want to be introduced as the host (e.g., "The Decorating Diva" or "Today's High-Tech Handyman," etc.)?

About Your Outro

1. Do you have examples of other podcast outros you like or dislike?
2. Do you have a specific call-to-action you want to include (e.g., subscribe on iTunes, sign up for our email list, Twitter/Facebook, etc.)?

About Your Music

1. Can you find some examples of music you like in an intro or outro?
2. Can you give a feel for the type of music you would like to have (rock, classical, etc.)?

Sometimes having a tangible, visual example can be the best way for a recipe to be the most useful. Two intros and outros from different podcasts targeting completely different avatars are presented to give you a balance of perspectives to consider.

Intro and Outro Script Examples

Onward Nation

Intro: *Get ready to find your recipe for success from America's top business owners here at* Onward Nation, *with your host, Stephen Woessner.*

Outro: *This episode is complete, so head over to OnwardNation.com for Show Notes and more food to fuel your ambition. Continue to find your recipe for success here at* Onward Nation.

Build a Better Agency

Intro: *If you're going to take the risk of running an agency, shouldn't you get the benefits, too? Welcome to* Build a Better Agency, *where we show you how to build an agency that can scale and grow with better clients, invested employees, and, best of all, more money to the bottom line. Bringing his twenty-five+ years of expertise as both an agency owner and agency consultant to you, please welcome your host, Drew McLellan.*

Outro: *That's all for this episode of* Build a Better Agency. *Be sure to visit AgencyManagementInstitute.com to learn more about our workshops and other ways we serve small to midsized agencies. While you're there, sign up for our e-newsletter, grab our free e-book, and check out the blog. Growing a bigger, better agency that makes more money, attracts bigger clients, and doesn't consume your life is possible, here on* Build a Better Agency.

Episode Flow

Now that you have your intro and outro completed, you're ready to move on to making decisions regarding the overall structure and flow of your episodes. For example, will you want to include a midroll? Will you want to announce your episode number to signify the beginning of each episode? Will you be recording solocasts or always episodes where you are interviewing a guest?

There are no right or wrong answers to those questions. Simply considering them will allow you to create the right experience for your listeners.

Caution: I strongly recommend that your initial ten episodes do not include any of the bells and whistles we are about to cover. For your initial ten, concentrate on the intro, editing and producing a high-quality interview and inserting it after the intro, and then inserting your outro at the close of the interview. This will help keep the editing as straightforward as possible while you learn the system. The simplicity will also help you focus on the episode flow. Then, after doing several recordings, you can decide what you want to add. Experiment with extra elements after Episode 10. Building a profitable podcast is a complex project. The initial simplicity will help you launch quickly and smoothly.

Here are some possible segments to consider. Think of these as little audio modules. Each module should have an audio pause before and after it begins for editing. For example, the host announces the episode number. Then pauses. Then introduces the guest. Then pauses. Then records the first half of the show. Then pauses. Then records the second half of the show. Then pauses.

Pausing is critical through the recording of an interview. You can always edit out a pause. However, it is extremely difficult, if not impossible, to add a pause into the middle of a conversation without it sounding awkward.

Definitions

Episode number: This is not a requirement. Announce the episode number as part of the recording only if you know the number and it has been added to your airing schedule.

Intro: This is prerecorded and edited. All you need to do is give a pause in the audio so you or your team can later edit it into your episodes.

Sound effect: With an audio pause in the right place, you can opt to edit in a sound effect. While this isn't common, it's certainly possible.

Sub-Intro: This is recorded in your own voice. While the intro will stay the same for a long time, the sub-intro is something that could be changed every ten episodes, especially if you are promoting a webinar or free download. A good sub-intro would be something like "Remember! If you go to [my podcast's website] before July 31st, you can download a free guide that will help you to X-Y-Z!" This is a limited-time call-to-action (CTA). This CTA can be for something you want to offer to grow your list, or a CTA for a sponsor. You decide. Again, this is optional.

First half of show: This is where you dive into your episode and then choose a place about halfway through to add a pause. You can introduce this pause. ("And now a word from our sponsors! *Pause*" for example.) Or, simply add a silent pause. Remember, you can always remove dead air, but you can't add it to conversation without it sounding awkward.

Midroll: This is traditionally where you insert a commercial from a sponsor. But you don't have to. You could exclude a midroll, or you could promote something of your own in this position. The midroll is similar to the sub-intro—a place to put a semi-temporary CTA and then replace it with another prerecorded audio when you want to change up your offer.

Second half of show: This is just like the first half except when you end the second half, you will need to pause to give some dead air space so the pre-outro and/or the outro can be added. Then you can start chatting with your guest again with no issues or just end the call. You decide what you think provides your listeners with the right experience.

Pre-Outro: The pre-outro is essentially the same as the sub-intro or the midroll. It is a third spot to be able to place a CTA. You can think about a CTA that is not going to always be in place and put it here. This could be a monthly offering, a class that is starting, or perhaps a webinar you will be launching.

Solocast: As I mentioned earlier, a solocast is simply an episode you record without a guest. You can record on your own schedule, and the show can be about a topic of your choice. This is a chance for you to shine and share your thought leadership. Simply pick a topic you want to cover and go for it. Keep in mind: A solocast doesn't need to be just you. If you have a business partner and you want to record things together like Car Talk's Click and Clack, then go for it.

Example #1: Solocast Flow

- Podcaster talks, does own intro, no music
- Insert sound effect
- Intro (prerecorded and edited)
- The whole podcast
- Podcaster talks, does own outro, CTA, no music
- Outro (prerecorded and edited)

Example #2: Guest Interview Flow

- Podcaster announces episode number (optional)
- Intro (prerecorded and edited)
- Sub-intro (introduce guest; recorded by podcaster) (CTA prerecorded) (optional)
- First half of show
- Midroll (CTA recorded by podcaster; recommended to treat a product or your company as a sponsor) (optional) (prerecorded)
- Second half of show
- Pre-outro (CTA recorded by podcaster) (prerecorded) (optional)
- Outro (prerecorded and edited)

CTA examples: subscribe, email me, call me, download X, rate and review, purchase product, or purchase book.

This is how example #2 would work:

- Episode number . . . pause.
- Guest introduction . . . pause.
- Then start in with episode. Do first half.

- Pause and introduce midroll.
- Pause and continue interview.
- End the interview with some dead air so the pre-outro and outro can be added later.
- Then continue chatting with your guest about anything that will not be part of the episode anymore.

How to Prepare for an Interview

Below are some brief recommendations for how to prepare for and conduct a professional interview with your guests. This should be modified based on the episode flow you select from the recipes in the preceding section.

1. Write down or print out a small script to use for introducing your guest.

2. Make sure you and the guest have added each other as Skype contacts.

3. Break down the guest's name phonetically and spell it out in your script in a way you can easily pronounce so you don't make a mistake during your introduction. Here's a tip: Go to YouTube to hear someone else introduce your guest! For instance: "Stephen Woessner" is pronounced "Stee-ven Wess-ner." Otherwise, you might accidentally say "Steff-en Whoaz-ner."

4. Prepare your show script/interview questions/interview flow, that is, the guide you will use to walk your way through the interview. I recommend storing this in Google Drive or some other location where you can easily access the file.

5. Customize the Show Notes for the guest you will be interviewing with the following:

   - Your introduction for your guests. This should be the bio they provided while booking the interview. Also add in any products or services they want pitched, which, again, they will have provided when they registered.

▸ The date the episode will be airing. Everyone wants to know. This should be in your Airing Schedule document. You don't need to have this in your recording, but your guests will likely ask at the beginning of the interview.

▸ The episode number. Here is a chance to make guests feel special as new guests (or impressed by your experience, depending on how many episodes you have produced).

▸ A request to promote the podcast. Let your guests know you would be grateful if they shared the episode when it airs. Most are delighted to promote their episode as a great way to share their wisdom with their nations of fans, who then become your concentric circles of lesser fans. Awesome, right?

6. Use this as an opportunity to talk to your guest about business! Remember, these are your Dream 50 prospects. The interview is your "all access pass," so make the most of it!

7. Open your Airing Schedule and keep it open throughout the interview. As you conduct the interview, you can then say things like: "Oh! That is so insightful! That reminds me of some advice [name of past guest] gave back in Episode [number of episode]! So when have you used this method in a powerful way?" You will sound like you have all the information of all your guests memorized. You, too, can sound like an information wizard with that simple trick. Bam!

8. Split your screen so your browser (housing your script and Airing Schedule documents in different tabs) is on one side of your computer screen and the Skype box on the other side of the screen. Keep your Skype window open enough to see your guest's first name. I know this may seem odd, but there will be times when you will have a brain freeze and cannot remember the name of the guest you are speaking with. So have it in your show script and in the Skype window. That way you never

end up like the rock singer who says: "Hey, Detroit! So happy to be here!" when the band's actually playing a gig in St. Louis. Ouch!

9. Have your recording software toolbar visible between the two applications so you can easily start the recording when you need to.

10. Do a test call! Skype lets you check that your mic and headset are working properly during a test call. Do this before every interview! If you notice a problem, go to Skype's settings, then to audio & video, and change the input and output for your audio to your headset or appropriate devices.

11. Dial up your guest on Skype.

12. Click the "record" button as soon as your guest answers. This prevents you from having an engaging pre-interview chat and then rolling into the actual interview, and forgetting to turn on the recorder. Not awesome.

13. When the interview is finished, be sure to leave some dead air for a few seconds before you begin your post-interview chat. The dead space is an edit point for your team.

14. Continue the conversation. Thank your guest for investing the time. This is an opportunity to build rapport and potentially open business conversations.

15. Fill out your Airing Schedule with the name of the guest, mark that the interview is completed, and let your team know where to find the audio file so they can edit it. Also, if you have a preference for the episode airing date or episode number, put it in the correct row on the document so your team remains informed.

iTunes Categories and Subcategories

iTunes represents approximately 60 percent of all podcast downloads. In a later chapter we will cover the process for getting your podcast into iTunes. But for now, I simply want you to review the titles of the sixteen main categories and their subcategories so you can decide where your podcast best fits. Libsyn permits you to select up to three iTunes categories for your show. The categories could be a main category like "Business"—or—a subcategory like "Careers." The subcategories tend to be a bit less competitive if part of your strategy happens to be scoring a high ranking as quickly as possible in your eight weeks of New and Noteworthy inclusion. I will cover launch strategy in detail in Chapter 14.

Arts

1. Design
2. Fashion & Beauty
3. Food
4. Literature
5. Performing Arts
6. Visual Arts

Business

1. Business News
2. Careers
3. Investing
4. Management & Marketing
5. Shopping

Comedy

Education

1. Educational Technology
2. Higher Education
3. K–12

4. Language Courses
5. Training

Games & Hobbies

1. Automotive
2. Aviation
3. Hobbies
4. Other Games
5. Video Games

Government & Organizations

1. Local
2. National
3. Nonprofit
4. Regional

Health

1. Alternative Health
2. Fitness & Nutrition
3. Self-Help
4. Sexuality

Kids & Family

. . . .

Music

. . . .

News & Politics

. . . .

Religion & Spirituality

. . . .

1. Buddhism
2. Christianity
3. Hinduism
4. Islam
5. Judaism
6. Other
7. Spirituality

Science & Medicine

. . . .

1. Medicine
2. Natural Sciences
3. Social Sciences

Society & Culture

. . . .

1. History
2. Personal Journals
3. Philosophy
4. Places & Travel

Sports & Recreation

. . . .

1. Amateur
2. College & High School
3. Outdoor
4. Professional
5. TV & Film

Technology

. . . .

1. Gadgets
2. Podcasting
3. Software How-To
4. Tech News

Look at you—zooming through the process!

Rock-solid awesome. Onward to Stage 4!

CHAPTER 11

STAGE 4:
SOCIAL MEDIA, RECORDING SOFTWARE, AND FIRST ROUND OF GUEST INTERVIEWS

This chapter covers the remaining system work you should complete before you schedule interviews with your first round of guests. For example, this is the ideal time to complete the remaining aspects of your social media strategy so you can make any necessary adjustments regarding the content you need to collect from guests to promote their episodes. Working through the process now will help you avoid having to go back to your guests and make a request—after you have already recorded the interview.

This chapter also covers the installation and setup of your recording software. It's a simple and efficient process, so you will be ready to begin recording your interviews in no time at all.

The largest chunk of this chapter is dedicated to the invitations you send to your guests. Your invitation is critical and must accomplish four important objectives:

1. Introduce the show and pique their interest in being a part of it.
2. Explain in detail how you will promote their episodes so they get some exposure—instead of the guests having to do all of the hard work.
3. Provide social proof either through links, videos, or a list of other guests you have interviewed.
4. Include a link to the podcast's online scheduling calendar so guests can book their interviews as effortlessly as possible.

We have provided an invitation template and examples so you can modify the content to fit your own style. You'll then have a top-notch invitation at the ready that will likely result in an 80 percent acceptance rate by your prospective guests.

Figure 11-1 illustrates the highlights of the production process in Stage 4.

The Stage 4 Project Sheet template (Figure 11-2) is available for your free download at PredictiveROI.com/resources/Stage-4. As with the earlier Project Sheets, it's a Google Sheet template so you can copy it into your Google Docs account and share it with all of the members of your team.

Recipe #1: Social Media Setup

I would like to start off by setting some expectations regarding your social media activity as it relates to your podcast. The recipe covered in this chapter is intended to augment your current social media strategy. This chapter is not intended to replace what you are currently doing on social media. Recipe #1 is specifically focused on sharing your guests' wisdom and encouraging your guests to share the content with their social media communities, all of which will expand your concentric circles of lesser fans.

You and your team will likely need one to two days to complete Stage 4.

FIGURE 11-1

4

This stage covers social media, recording software, and preparing for inviting your first guests.

EMAIL OUTLINING MATERIALS FOR STAGE 4

This email will be sent to you a week before our meeting. If it does not arrive, reach out to us or check your spam folder.

SOCIAL MEDIA

We will cover what social media each party will be doing, what it will be like, and the accesses we will need to do our work.

RECORDING SOFTWARE

This is a critical part of the setup. Your podcast is only as good as your recordings. We will be going through your settings, testing, and setting up a mock interview.

INVITING GUESTS

This can be a difficult and scary prospect for many, but we will provide the ingredients you need to reach out successfully to prospective guests.

DECIDE ON NEXT MEETING

Pick a time within 7 to 9 days to do the next meeting and get it on everyone's calendar.

POST MEETING FOLLOW-UP

Following the meeting you will get an email outlining what will need to be done before our next meeting.

Goal

Our goal during the meeting is to have you ready to start recording and inviting guests to be on your show and decide how social media will be covered by our respective teams.

FIGURE 11-2

STAGE 4	Company Name–Name of Podcast	
	Job/Task	Status/Questions
	Recipe 1: Social Media Setup	
Meeting	Social media post style/design approved	
Meeting	Twitter login confirmed:	
Meeting	Username	
Meeting	Password	
Meeting	Facebook login confirmed:	
Meeting	Username	
Meeting	Password	
Meeting	LinkedIn login confirmed:	
Meeting	Username	
Meeting	Password	
Meeting	Hootsuite login confirmed:	
Meeting	Username	
Meeting	Password	
Meeting	SocialOomph login confirmed:	
Meeting	Username	
Meeting	Password	
	Recipe 2: Set Up Recording Software	
Meeting	Skype installed and client can log in	
Email	Recording software installed and settings configured	
Meeting	Test the recording software–conduct mock interview	
Email/ video	Review Airing Schedule as destination for audio files	

FIGURE 11-2   (continued)

STAGE 2	Company Name–Name of Podcast	
	Job/Task	**Status/Questions**
	Recipe 3: Prepare Guest Invite	
Email	Guest invitation approved	
Email	Distribute invitation for first round of guests (not your Dream 50)	

SOCIAL MEDIA PROTOCOLS

This is the process we use for Twitter, Facebook, and LinkedIn.

We recommend connecting your social media profiles to a Hootsuite account to simplify the work and save time.

Twitter

We use Twitter in three ways:

◆ We post through Hootsuite on the day an episode airs. We recommend adding an image to each of these posts to help them stand out in your followers' feeds. Figure 11-3 is an example of an Air Day tweet.

FIGURE 11-3

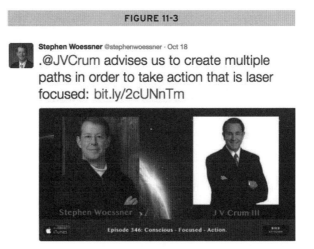

- We listen to the audio and create one tweet that highlights the wisdom a guest shared while answering each question during the interview. These tweets (which we then add to our Twitter library sheet) contain:

  - Content about the episode
  - The guest's Twitter handle
  - A link to the episode (shortened using "bit.ly")

- We compile the Air Day tweet, along with the nine other tweets written to support the episode, and load them into SocialOomph as a .txt file to reuse and recycle as part of our ongoing content-marketing library. We send one randomized tweet from our library every forty-two minutes. This strategy has helped us organically attract and engage with thousands of new followers. As Figure 11-3 shows, we include the Twitter handle of our guest, which encourages the like, reply, and re-tweet as in Figure 11-4.

FIGURE 11-4

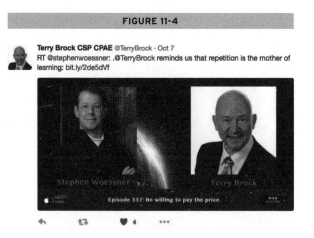

Facebook Posts

- We take the content from the show title field in the Airing Schedule. Then we match it to the Tweet that best represents that title. If none match, we create some new content. We remove the

Twitter handle. We massage that content to be clear and interesting (see Figure 11-5).

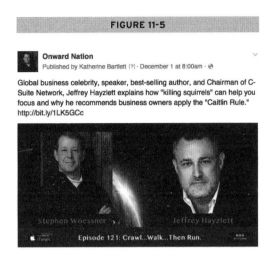

FIGURE 11-5

Onward Nation
Published by Katherine Bartlett [?] · December 1 at 8:00am · 🌐

Global business celebrity, speaker, best-selling author, and Chairman of C-Suite Network, Jeffrey Hayzlett explains how "killing squirrels" can help you focus and why he recommends business owners apply the "Caitlin Rule."
http://bit.ly/1LK5GCc

Episode 121: Crawl...Walk...Then Run.

- We take the image of the guest from ScheduleOnce and create the FB post image.
- We insert the copy and then the image into Hootsuite.
- We change the title of the post to match what is in the Airing Schedule.
- We schedule the posts on Hootsuite.

LinkedIn Posts
- We reuse the content from the Facebook posts.
- We post to LinkedIn, scheduling it for the same time as the FB posts.

DISTRIBUTION SCHEDULE
- Podcast audio goes live at 4 A.M. CST on Libsyn.
- New Episode Tweets will be posted between 8 and 9 A.M. in your time zone.
- Tweets go out at least once in the morning and once in the evening. At *Onward Nation*, our Tweet library has grown to nearly 3,500

tweets so we can send a new tweet every forty-two minutes and not repeat a tweet for weeks.

- FB posts go out between 8 and 9 A.M. CST.
- LinkedIn posts go out between 8 and 9 A.M. CST.

Recipe #2: Set Up Recording Software

You are very close to being ready to invite your first round of guests to schedule interviews. Working through the setup of your Skype account and installation of your recording software is an efficient process. But please complete this step, test it, conduct a mock interview, and then invite your guests to schedule an interview. You don't want to be installing software and testing Skype on the morning of your first interview.

My team and I created several brief tutorial videos that you can find at PredictiveROI.com/Stage-4 to help this recipe go as smoothly as possible.

This recipe is divided into three ingredients. Ingredient #1 covers what you will need to know about Skype as it relates to recording your interviews. You will connect with all of your guests via Skype to conduct the interviews.

Ingredient #2 is for you if you are using a Mac. Ingredient #3 is for you if you are using a PC. After Ingredient #1, and if you will be recording your interviews on a Mac, go to Ingredient #2. Or, go to Ingredient #3 if you will be recording your interviews on a PC.

INGREDIENT #1: SKYPE

You will need to install and learn how to use Skype regardless of whether you're using a Mac or PC.

Installation is easy. Go to https://www.skype.com/en/download-skype/skype-for-computer/ and be sure to select the version for either Mac or PC.

During installation, you will need to set up a profile if you do not already have one, or create a new one if you want your Skype account for your podcast to be different from your personal one.

Follow the instructions and keep an eye out for when it tries to make Bing your default browser (Skype is owned by Microsoft).

You can find more installation-specific directions from Skype here:

For PC: https://support.skype.com/en/faq/FA11098/how-do-i-download-and-install-skype-for-windows-desktop

ForMac: https://support.skype.com/en/faq/FA12015/getting-started-with-skype-for-mac

INGREDIENT #2: MAC

If you plan to record your podcast on a Mac, you'll be using a piece of software called Ecamm Call Recorder For Skype. This is a short section because the installation is efficient and the video tutorial we created for you in our Resources section visually demonstrates each of the steps if you would like an additional point of reference.

1. Go here: http://www.ecamm.com/mac/callrecorder/.
2. Click the "buy" button.
3. Pay with credit card if possible instead of PayPal.
4. Follow the instructions Ecamm provides for purchasing, accessing, and downloading the software.
5. Once you can start Ecamm on your computer, watch this video: https://drive.google.com/open?id=0B552kT0gTG8nY3ZMZEFqRWx4VVE.
6. If you run into any kind of trouble, let me know!

INGREDIENT #3: PC

If you are using a PC, you'll need to download and install a different call recorder. The software is called Pamela, and you can find it here: https://www.pamela.biz/.

We divided the installation process into three sections and created a tutorial video for each. You can find them here: PredictiveROI.com/Resources/Stage-4.

1. Downloading Pamela
2. Installing Pamela
3. Settings for Pamela

Recipe #3: Prepare Your Guest Invitation

For some business owners, the prospect of sending out invitations to their Dream 50 list of prospects can feel daunting. Plus, you are using new technology, new questions, and a new platform. Rest assured, this recipe will help reduce any potential anxiety you may be feeling by giving you a proven framework you can copy and begin using right away. These assets, along with confidence, are really all you need in order to book great guests on your show.

So how will you send out the guest invitation email?

1. Make sure you have your list of prospective interviewees handy.
2. Select those whom you feel you'll be comfortable interviewing and will provide good content. One or the other isn't a great choice. For instance, you may be very comfortable with your aunt Marge, but she probably lacks the subject matter expertise you want to share with your audience. Similarly, picking a subject-matter master whom you are afraid to interview will lead to an unsuccessful show.
3. Modify the email template to include something personal about each of the individuals you are emailing and why you think that person will do a good job.
4. Double-check that all the links within your email template are working.
5. Click "Send."
6. Don't expect an immediate response. This can be hard at first, but you are asking busy people to make time for you. You need to adopt the mindset of a salesperson. You are now in a sales process. You want these individuals to spend time on your show. Do follow-ups, keep asking, and be persistent.
7. As your list of aired interviews grows, you will begin receiving requests from prospective guests who want to be on your show. That is a very good feeling. Be sure to post your archive link some-place prominently within your invitation as well as on your website. Here's what *Onward Nation*'s looks like: http://onwardnation.com/podcast-archives/.

8. Figure 11-6 is a screenshot of what your invitation will look like as your guest opens it.

FIGURE 11-6

FIGURE 11-6

Chris . . . thank you for accepting my invitation to be on *Onward Nation* . . . am looking forward to our time together.

Here are some additional details . . .

Our interviews are conducted via Skype and are audio-only.

Attached are the questions I ask each guest—however—I will create a custom set of questions for you so we can be finished in twenty minutes.

We will promote your episode via:

1. Episode-specific email campaigns to our Predictive ROI list
2. Distribution across our three Facebook profiles
3. Posts to my LNKD connections
4. Posts to my Twitter followers
5. Targeted ads on Facebook to drive traffic to your "Show Notes" page at OnwardNation.com
6. Your "Show Notes" page will include highlights from your interview as well as include links to resources, etc., that you suggest/recommend during our discussion.

You can learn more about my background from the video interview that Darren Hardy and I did at: **https://youtu.be/Mg5J_ZGJazY**.

You can schedule your interview at: **http://www.meetme.so/OnwardNation**.

I am thrilled to have you on the show, Chris!

Sincerely Yours,
Stephen Woessner
Host of The Onward Nation Podcast
CEO of Predictive ROI
M: 608-498-5165

Template: Guest Invitation

The invitation template includes several critical ingredients to help establish credibility and "social proof" in the hearts and minds of your prospective guests—and to assure them that being a guest on your show will expand their own platforms. Let's dive deeper into both.

The first three sentences following "Here are the details to consider" are all designed as credibility indicators. Including the number of countries where your podcast is listened to (even if the number is 10) let your guest know you are building an international reach. My team and I tested this message on Facebook when *Onward Nation* reached 83 countries, and we received some wonderful comments. As soon as we reached 100 countries we made it an even bigger deal. I now include "200 countries" in all of our invitations.

Include a link to the names of all your past guests and their interviews. Guests may recognize some names and may even listen to a few snippets of some of your interviews. This is another excellent credibility indicator.

And speaking of credibility indicators, if you have a video of you being interviewed by someone else, the invitation is a perfect place to add it. When I sent out my first several invitations for *Onward Nation*, we had zero international exposure and we did not have an archive of interviews with past guests. But what I did have—and what I included a link to—was a rockin' awesome video of Darren Hardy (who at the time was the publisher of *SUCCESS Magazine*), interviewing me about money-draining mistakes most business owners make. Have you ever been interviewed regarding your areas of expertise? If so, include the link within the invitation.

The credibility indicators will have done their job if your prospective guest reads on. So now I would like to direct your attention to the five bullet points toward the middle of the invitation. These are the "platform-building" bullets that tell your prospective guests how you will promote their episodes and drive more traffic your way. Yes, you want their help in promoting the episode—and most of your guests will go out of their way to help you. But being a guest on your show will begin to feel like a lot of work on their part if you don't articulate how you will bring an audience to them.

It has been our experience that the size of the email list behind a show provides guests with assurance that the host has some marketing horsepower behind him or her. The email list doesn't need to have 100,000 names. Even several thousand highly targeted email subscribers will be impressive to most guests. And be sure to revise the number in your invitation upward as your email list grows.

The bullet points should also include your plan for social media distribution.

The following template is the core of what we have used at *Onward Nation* to book interviews with hundreds of today's top business owners. In addition, all of our podcasting clients at Predictive ROI are using modified variations of this same invitation. It works extremely well.

Please note: Any content bolded in the template should be revised to fit your show.

> Subject: [Podcast Name] Invitation
>
> Good Morning [Guest], I hope you are doing well. [I really enjoyed our conversation several years ago—wow—time flies by].
>
> I would be honored, [Guest], if you joined me as my guest on our top-ranked daily podcast for business owners called [Podcast Name].
>
> Here are the details to consider . . .
>
> [Podcast Name] is listened to in [XXX] countries.
>
> You can find our full guest list here: [Link to archive page on your podcast website.]
>
> You can learn more about my background from the video interview that Darren Hardy (former publisher of *SUCCESS Magazine*) and I did at: https://youtube/Mg5J_ZGJazY.
>
> The interviews are conducted via [Connection platform being used (e.g., Skype, Zoom, GTM, etc.)] and are audio-only.
>
> Attached are the questions I ask each guest. [Link to questions list]
>
> Each interview lasts approximately [Time in minutes].

We will promote your episode via:

- Episode-specific email campaigns to our [Specific number of people on your email list] email list
- Distribution on our Facebook profile
- Posts to my LNKD connections
- Posts to my Twitter followers
- Targeted ads on Facebook to drive traffic to your "Show Notes" page at [Podcast Name]

Your Show Notes page will include highlights from your interview as well as include links to resources, etc., that you suggest/recommend during our discussion.

If you are interested, you can schedule your interview at: [Link to Schedule-Once booking page].

I would be thrilled to have you on the show!

Your thoughts, [Guest First Name]?

Show Them You're Serious

An excellent confidence-building strategy is to record your initial set of ten interviews, launch your show, and then begin reaching out to invite members of your Dream 50 list to join you as a guest on your show. Social proof is critically important: Your show being live, receiving reviews in iTunes, social media posts being distributed, and your archive of interviews beginning to fill up are all excellent credibility indicators that you are serious about your show. Then, accepting your invitation is an easy "yes" for your Dream 50.

✓ SOCIAL MEDIA AND RECORDING CHECKLIST ✓

❏ Identify two to three pieces of social proof you can include within your invitation to a prospective guest.

❏ Customize the invitation template provided in this chapter to save you some time.

❏ Review the posting/airing schedule for social media and episodes with your team to make sure everyone is on the same page.

❏ Set up and test your recording software by conducting a mock interview with a member of your team via Skype.

❏ Record your first round of ten interviews so you have ample inventory when you launch your podcast.

CHAPTER 12

STAGE 5:
FINAL WEBSITE CONTENT
AND SHOW NOTES

The pre-launch production of your podcast is quickly coming to an end. Soon your vital priorities will switch to romancing your Dream 50, promoting your show with excellence and tenacity, and selling! But before we tackle new priorities, you need to select a Show Notes template for your podcast website, consider several guest-friendly content pages for your website, and set up your Libsyn account along with your distribution linkages into iTunes, Stitcher, and Google Play.

We have included easy-to-download templates for the Show Notes, FAQs, and About Host content pages at PredictiveROI.com/Resources/Stage-5.

Figure 12-1 illustrates the highlights of the production process in Stage 5.

Bonus Training: Being an Infusionsoft subscriber is not a requirement for creating a successful podcast. However, if you are looking to take your guest advocacy system to the highest level of automation, then you will want to visit PredictiveROI.com/Resources/Stage-5 for our comprehensive (free) tutorial on best practices. The tutorials include Infusionsoft campaigns to help ensure that

FIGURE 12-1

5

These are final pieces for your website build and preparation for ranking well in iTunes.

EMAIL OUTLINING MATERIALS FOR STAGE 5

This email will be sent to you a week before our kickoff meeting. If it does not arrive, reach out to us or check your spam folder.

WEBSITE CONTENT

Everything from your FAQ page to your bio and podcast description. This is where we hash out the website content.

SHOW NOTES

This is all about how you want to have your episodes described, how long you want them, and what they should contain.

GETTING REVIEWS

Reviews are not like the Field of Dreams. We want to take an active role in getting reviews for your podcast, and this is how we will do it.

DECIDE ON NEXT MEETING

Pick a time within 7 to 9 days to do the next meeting and get it on everyone's calendar.

POST MEETING FOLLOW-UP

Following the meeting you will get an email outlining what will need to be done before our next meeting.

Goal

This is really the final run up to launch. At this point the only thing we will be working through is loose ends and getting recordings as needed before launch.

revenue-generating opportunities with your guests are captured. Our online Resources library is continually updated in order to keep pace with the new features at Infusionsoft and ScheduleOnce. Our tutorials cover topics such as:

- How to integrate Infusionsoft with ScheduleOnce
- How to create guest advocacy campaigns in Infusionsoft
- How to tag guests in Infusionsoft upon registration
- How to create and distribute marketing automation campaigns to your guests
- How to build and edit lists
- How to build and embed Infusionsoft forms into your podcast website forms
- And much more

The Stage 5 Project Sheet template (Figure 12-2, p.146–147) is available for your free download at PredictiveROI.com/resources/Stage-5. As with the earlier Project Sheets, it is a Google Sheet template so you can copy it into your Google Docs account and share it with all of the members of your team.

Completing Stage 5 should take you and your team one or two days.

Recipe #1: Documents for Review

INGREDIENT #1: SHOW NOTES TEMPLATES

You or your team should write a "Show Notes" summary highlighting each episode's key lessons or discussion points. Think of your Show Notes as an individual blog post created to house each of your episodes on your podcast website. A Show Notes page is not a full transcript of the episode; it is just enough information to pique the reader's interest in listening to the full episode.

We typically produce Show Notes for clients using one of two templates: Style A (Bullets) or Style B (Q&A). Using an A/B template will save a lot of time. Your clients will be able to listen to the recording, take notes, jump from question to question, select a highlight, and then move on to the next section in the Show Notes.

FIGURE 12-2

Stage 5	Client Name–Name of Podcast		
	Job/Task	Status/Questions	Example Assets
Documents For Review–Stage #5			
Meeting	What style of Show Notes would you like?		-
Meeting	Approve FAQ page		
Meeting	Approve host biography		
Meeting	Approve podcast description		
Meeting	Approve "Request for Review" email		
Loose Ends–Stage #5			
Meeting	Need logo for ScheduleOnce page		
Meeting	Is this Gmail being redirected to any other email account?		
Meeting	What is the email it will redirect toward?		
Meeting	Redirect complete		
Meeting	List of 60–75 people who will rate and review you within first two weeks of launch		-
Meeting	Dream 50 list completed		-
Do Before Meeting–Stage #5			
Internal	Launch email written		
Internal	Launch email approved		
Internal	Write podcast description if needed		

FIGURE 12-2 (continued)

Libsyn, iTunes, Stitcher, and HootSuite—Stage #5			
	Job/Task	**Status/Questions**	**Example Assets**
Internal After Meeting	Create Stitcher account		
Internal After Meeting	Create Libsyn account		
Internal After Meeting	Create iTunes account		
Internal After Meeting	Connect iTunes and Stitcher to Libsyn		
Internal After Meeting	Hootsuite connection confirmed		

Productivity Tip: Encourage your team to create hidden placeholder pages in the podcast website for each upcoming episode once you decide on the template/style of Show Notes. For example, your team could have twenty fully completed episodes "in the can." They would include audio edited and uploaded to Libsyn and scheduled for distribution, Show Notes created for each episode and scheduled in WordPress to match up with the Libsyn air dates, and social media posts preloaded/scheduled into Hootsuite and SocialOomph. When your team can put this predictable and repeatable system into place, it will begin to feel as though your podcast were running on autopilot. Working ahead like this helps you, as the host and business owner, shift your attention toward developing relationships with your Dream 50.

Style A Show Notes: Bullets

Episode Title, with Guest's Full Name

You can find an example here: http://buildabetteragency.com/scott-monty/.

The first paragraph in your Show Notes introduces the guest, regardless of Show Notes format. Typically, three to seven sentences long, this is most often the bio that the guest provides, either via ScheduleOnce or through email. If this episode is a solocast, then we're talking about your bio.

What you'll learn about in this episode:

- Topic 1
- Topic 2
- Topic 3
- Etc.—through every topic discussed in the episode

Ways to Contact [Guest's First Name]:

- Website
- Email
- Twitter
- Etc.—Whatever your guest provides

Predictive ROI Note: The biggest advantage to Style A is that it is the shortest template. It showcases what each episode offers rather than giving it away in text. This urges anyone reading your Show Notes page to take the next step and listen to the episode. This is our recommended format for most podcasts.

Style B Show Notes: Q&A

Episode Title, with Guest's Full Name

You can find an example here: http://onwardnation.com/jay-baer/.

As with Style A, the first paragraph in your Show Notes introduces the guest in a three-to-seven-sentence bio.

Following the first paragraph, this style of Show Notes will feature every question from your official question list and the answers your guest provides.

Example:

A question could be:

Is there a secret, time-saving technique that helps you focus and tackle your most vital priorities each day?

We could put that exact question into the Show Notes or abbreviate it as:

Secret time-saving technique

And then the answer would follow. This style would repeat for every question in your question list.

Ways to Contact [Guest's First Name]:

♦ Website
♦ Email
♦ Twitter
♦ Etc.—Whatever your guest provides

Predictive ROI Note: Style B is intended for podcasts that will use the same questions week-to-week.

INGREDIENT #2: PODCAST WEBSITE CONTENT PAGE FAQS

You can find an example here: http://focusisyourfriend.com/faq/.

Thank you so much for agreeing to be a guest on [Podcast Name]. I absolutely cannot wait to speak with you. But first, here's everything you need to know to make sure our conversation can happen without any mishaps—technological or otherwise.

[*Podcast Name*] is focused on [Description of podcast].

Schedule Your Interview

Please click the link below to schedule your interview. I normally record interviews at specific times, but I can be flexible if need be. If none of the times on the schedule work for you, shoot me an email at [Email Address], and we'll work something out.

[Schedule your interview button]

What I Need from You

When you schedule your interview through the above link, I'm going to need the following information from you:

1. Name
2. Email
3. Company Name
4. Role in Company
5. Website
6. Twitter Handle (makes sure we connect with the right person/account via social media)
7. Skype Handle (helps you connect on Skype)
8. Phone Number
9. Mailing Address (for mailing thank yous, future communications, or gifts)
10. Links to whatever you would like us to promote in your Show Notes page
11. Guest bio (for the website and use as an intro)
12. Headshot (for website and social media)

The Interview

We will record our interview on Skype, and it'll take about forty-five to sixty minutes of your time, depending on how in-depth we get with our conversation. We'll talk for a few minutes before we start the recording so that we can get to know each other a little bit and check the sound. I'll also answer any questions you might have, and I'll have you pronounce your name for me. After that, we'll begin the recording.

Technical Details

[*Podcast Name*] is an audio-only podcast, recorded on Skype. If you do not have a Skype account, please sign up for a free one by clicking here and downloading the software to your computer. My Skype name is [Skype Name], and you'll need to add me to your contact list. I will call you via Skype at the time that we've scheduled for our interview.

To make sure our interview sounds great, please review my sound guide PDF. [Sound Guide: Click Here]

You'll also need to:

- Sit in a quiet place for the interview (e.g., not a coffee shop).
- Silence your phone(s).
- Connect Skype to your headset/microphone.
- Silence your Skype notifications (here's how: Windows and Mac [include links]).
- Turn off other on-screen applications that might be running on your computer.
- Use a headset with a built-in microphone or a stand-alone mic with earbuds.

Interview Promotion

After our interview, I will promote your podcast episode extensively on social media and through my email list. I encourage you to do the same thing. Promotion on your part isn't a requirement for being a guest, but I highly recommend that you bring our interview to your audience's attention. I've created a guide to help with that, which you can download here [Download link]. The day before your episode airs, you will be sent links for all of your episode information.

Thanks, and I can't wait to speak with you!

INGREDIENT #3: DESCRIPTION FOR ITUNES

There are two options for how to complete this section on preparing your description that will be displayed in iTunes (see Figure 12-3).

FIGURE 12-3

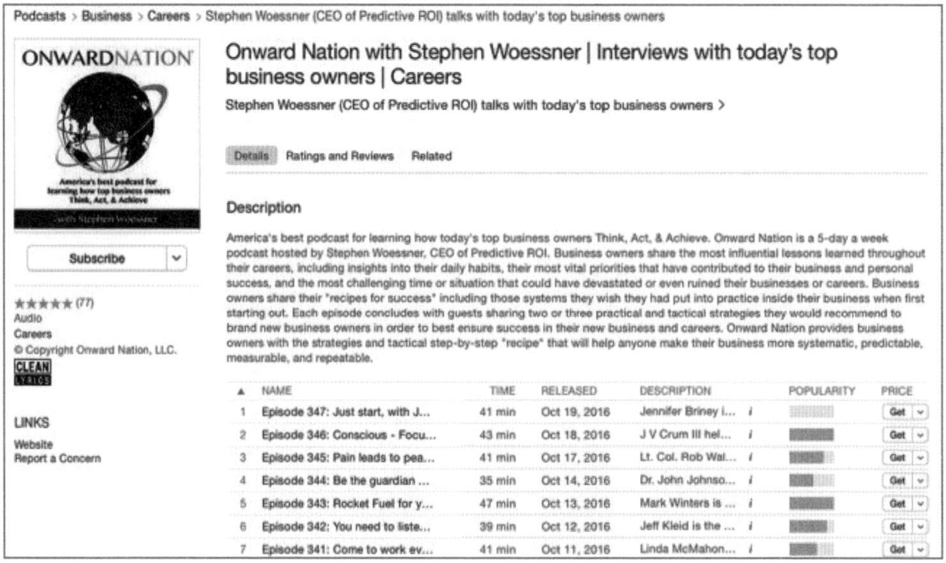

- ◆ Write down, in your own words, what you think is the right description for the podcast. Explain what you hope to achieve and why people should listen. Ultimately, you'll answer the question for readers of, "What's in it for me?"
- ◆ Simply record your thoughts and goals for the podcast and what people will be getting out of it. Our team will then take that audio and pull it apart to write a podcast description for you to review.

Recipe #2: Libsyn, iTunes, Stitcher, and Google Play Setup

Your final step before recording your interview is to set up your Libsyn account so it is ready for you to upload your completed episodes. Hosting more than 25,000 podcasts, Libsyn has been a leading podcast-hosting company over the past ten years. At the time of this writing, we have produced, uploaded, and distributed nearly 1,000 episodes through Libsyn and have never had a single problem. We've never even had to connect with their support department. Their platform is *that* stable!

You may be asking yourself, "Why do I need a podcast host if I want my episodes to be available inside iTunes?" Excellent question. I wondered the same thing when we were working through the *Onward Nation* launch process.

Libsyn is where you will upload, store, or "host" all of your audio files (your episodes). When each upload is complete, Libsyn will give you a URL for where you can find the episode. For example, you can find my interview with Gary Vaynerchuk here in Libsyn: http://traffic.libsyn.com/onwardnation/ Gary_Vaynerchuk_Interview.mp3. Or, you can find the same interview at On-wardNation.com/Gary-Vaynerchuk. Either way, it's the same audio file. The only difference: OnwardNation.com is pulling the audio file from Libsyn into our website to give it a better presentation. But the content is still coming from Libsyn.

Plus, with each episode you upload, Libsyn will automatically update the RSS feed for your show. Your podcast will run on an RSS feed similar to a blog. When a new episode is available in Libsyn, and the publishing day and time you set inside Libsyn has arrived, Libsyn will add your latest episode to your RSS feed. Once added, your latest episode will quickly appear in iTunes, Stitcher, and Google Play because your RSS feed is a new immediate conduit of content into those platforms.

Setting up your Libsyn account is simple. We created a step-by-step tutorial for setting it up: PredictiveROI.com/Resources/Stage-5.

And PredictiveROI.com/Resource/Launch includes tutorials on how to set up your iTunes, Stitcher, and Google Play accounts. However, don't set up those accounts until you're ready to launch. That's because once you provide iTunes with your RSS feed, it's out of your hands; iTunes will immediately get to work in creating your iTunes channel and making your content available in its directory. That's why setting up iTunes, Stitcher, and Google Play are part of our launch recipe.

For now, please create your Libsyn account and then move on to Stage 6 to master all things audio.

CHAPTER 13

STAGE 6:
EQUIPMENT, SOFTWARE, AND EDITING YOUR INTERVIEWS

This chapter will provide you with specific equipment recommendations so you can begin recording the audio for your episodes for less than $300. We're also including our full audio editing recipe so you can follow the same process used by our Predictive ROI team. We will cover how to record each interview, where to save the recorded files, and how to edit an interview into an episode using Adobe Audition. When you finish this chapter, you'll be ready to produce your first episode and upload into iTunes for the whole world to hear!

Equipment Overview

Business owners might actually be surprised to find out that they don't need an expensive studio to create an awesome podcast. It's also easy to fall into the mental trap of thinking all the equipment is going to be confusing to hook up in a certain way, but I'm going to share a simple list you can just purchase from Amazon.

To start off, you will need a computer—it doesn't matter if it's a PC or a Mac. But I strongly recommend a computer with a lot of memory.

Invest in an external hard drive to save all your audio, because whether you are doing one, three, or five episodes a week, you are going to be using up a lot of memory on your computer.

It's better to get an external hard drive, so you can store all that audio and all of your edits on there.

You will also need editing software. There are several options to consider, including:

- Adobe Audition
- GarageBand
- Audacity

If you want to use a free version, go with Audacity.

At the time of this writing we have used Adobe Audition—on which the editing checklist in this chapter is based—to edit nearly 1,000 episodes. It is awesome and a good investment. The monthly cost is approximately $20 through Adobe's Creative Cloud.

You'll need to purchase a tool that helps remove the echo in your audio. It is called DeVerberate. You can buy it from Acon Digital for about $100. You can find it here: https://acondigital.com/products/deverberate/.

Most important, you will need a high-quality microphone. At *Onward Nation*, we use the Audio-Technica 2100, or ATR 2100 for short. You can find it on Amazon for around $80. But you definitely need a microphone. Do not try to record your episodes using your computer's built-in mic.

Recording and Editing

Let's say that I interview a guest on Skype, and because I'm using a Mac, I installed the Ecamm Call Recorder, which is a onetime $30 expense. It works like a plug-in that bolts onto Skype so whenever I open Skype to connect with a guest, Ecamm automatically opens and is ready to record. And when my guest and I end our Skype session, and I close down Skype, Ecamm captures the audio and saves it directly into my *Onward Nation* Dropbox folder. Then my team can grab the audio file and begin the editing process.

Stay organized by getting in the habit of creating folders with your guest name as the title of each folder. It's pretty basic. Just go to your external hard drive and create a simple folder you'll call "Joe Smith." Then, you'll take your audio file from your interview and put it in Joe Smith's folder. Then open your Adobe Audition, and once that is up, you'll place the file for your interview into your left window where it says "Files."

Then, simply go up to "Edit" at the top of the window and click "Split into Mono Files." You are going to want to do this, because if you are recording correctly, you should end up with a "dual track" where you have your voice at the top and your guest's voice at the bottom.

This will be awesome, because then you can go into that file and touch up the voices and make sure everything sounds clean. You can go in there and fix the audio track. When you do that, just make sure you split it into mono files. Your audio files should either say "Joe Smith left" or "Joe Smith right." It's going to split that up or it's going to say "one" and "two," but you'll be able to tell which "one" is your audio and which is your guest's audio.

Once that is split up, remove anything before your introduction to the episode. I tend to begin *Onward Nation* episodes with, "Good Morning, *Onward Nation*, I'm Stephen Woessner." So that is my team's audio cue: Delete everything before that marker, such as chitchat with guests.

Also, you should apply your noise reduction. Remove annoying static. That's key to just a nice, clean audio. Here's how: Go to your "Effects" and then go to "Noise Reduction." Once you are there, select an area right before you start speaking in your podcast. Before you speak in your audio track, before you say, "Hello. This is my podcast," you are going to want to take a sample of your audio, copy it, and then select your whole audio to get rid of that static.

Once you are done with static, locate the volume tool on your track and lower the volume during the silences when your guest isn't talking.

Also be sure of your own audio wave as the host. Suppose you hear yourself saying, "Aah" or "Mm-hmm"—you may want to edit that out. If you do, just be aware: You don't want to accidentally get rid of the part after the "Mm-hmm" where you said, "Yeah. I definitely agree with your answer," or something else that's relevant.

Once you are done going through the whole track, go to the "Effects" menu. Select "VST." Then right-click your mouse. It's going to read "VST" a couple of times.

That's where you will find the DeVerberate tool you purchased. Click De-Verberate to open it. Once you do, you will see a window pop up. There are going to be some dials. One setting reads, "Reduce Ambiance" at the top. Just make sure that's your setting. The dials on the bottom left are where you will change your echo.

Be a little sensitive in this area. Try not to make yourself sound like you're in a tube. If you are left with a little bit of an echo, don't freak out. It's going to be better than when you first had the audio.

Next, reapply "Match Loudness," or if you have an older version of Adobe Audition, use "Match Volume."

Now it's time to lower your volume down to -16 LUFS. This level is an ideal setting for a podcast. It's the standard.

Then you apply the same recipe to your guest's audio.

When listening to your guest's audio, listen for the part where you know they're saying, "Thank you for having me on the show," which represents the start of the interview. Delete everything before that. Then, go through and apply the noise reduction tool again, finding that one piece where it's just static. Copy that, and select the whole file. Apply it so it gets rid of all that static. Then go through and delete the waves of audio that are just little noises. Even on the guest's end, you might hear them clicking or tapping on the desk, or drinking a glass of water. We've heard—and gotten rid of—a lot of things that come through on the guest's end.

After the noise reduction process, don't apply the DeVerberate tool right away. I find that it's better to wait until the "Multitrack" stage in Audition.

Next, just do the "Match Loudness" or "Match Volume" and go to -16 LUFS again. We'll have the screenshot for all the settings on how you get to -16 LUFS.

The good news is that you're done with the hard part!

The entire process should take you about thirty to forty-five minutes.

Once you have all that together, take a look at your Multitrack session. It should read, "Host, Interview, Sound Effects, Music Bed, and Master." You're going to want to go into your "Effects Rack" on the left. Once there, go to "Track Effects." For your Master, Interview, and Host rows, turn off all the effects. We find this easier because, depending on the quality of your guest's audio compared to yours, there may be obvious differences so, ideally, keep them the same level. Sometimes if you have your audio very advanced and your guest's audio is different, there might have been some connect troubles. Your audience is going to be able to tell, so it is best to keep them similar, at the same level, same effects.

Once you've removed those, take a look at your left panel and double-check again that you have all your files. Then go ahead and set your audio file into the host—because you are a host. Then set your guest into the interview row, and then set your intro into the sound effects. It is okay to keep your track effects in the sound effects, because you probably had a professional make them, and, thus, their files are likely compatible with that.

Once you have your intro into the row, and you have all your other audio pieces in there, you're going to want to fit them like a puzzle, because the pieces are not going to be perfectly aligned. Take a listen to make sure that your audio is falling into the same place when you are talking, as when your guest is speaking.

Go ahead and line that up. You may notice delays when you are looking through your audio, say maybe a few five-second pauses. Double-check those pauses; if there is some sort of awkward pause in between conversations, cut it.

You will see the eraser tool at the top left. It looks like an actual eraser. You can go through and give your audio a nice cut with your mouse. Select both rows and move the eraser over them. Just take your time with this, so you make sure that everything continues to follow through.

Once you've gone through and made those cuts, select all the audio that you have in there. With "Command A," all your audio is going to be selected—and you can listen at up to +65 percent speed and take out cell phone rings, reminder beeps, lags, glitches, and other extraneous noises.

Unfortunately, depending on how bad the glitch or lag is, you might not be able to remove it. If you don't want to seek out professional help for the fix, be sure you let your guest know.

Once you have listened to all of it at that speed, click all of your audio again. Stretch it back to 100 percent.

Once it is back to normal, you can go to your "Mixdown Session" and then to "New File" and click "Entire Session." This might take a minute depending on how big your file is, but just give it a minute. Once it's all mixed together, you will be able to "Export" the file.

The file name is going to read "Mixdown 1." Delete the "Mixdown 1" and leave the name you gave it originally. That's going to end up on your desktop, and you just throw it into your Google Drive, which is what we use, and put it into Libsyn.

If you're new to this, editing an entire episode could take a couple of hours. But once you have it down, you should be able to edit an hour podcast in sixty minutes. For a thirty-minute show, editing should take only thirty minutes.

✓ YOUR AUDIO EDITING CHECKLIST ✓

❑ **1.** Create a folder on your computer desktop and name it using your guest's name (Example: Joe Smith).

❑ **2.** Place your recorded audio file from your interview (.mov file) into the guest folder.

❑ **3.** Open Adobe Audition.

❑ **4.** Import .mov file into Adobe Audition.

❑ **5.** Select the .mov file, go to "Edit," then to "Split into Mono Files."

❑ **6.** Keep your audio (as the host) on an L (1) and the audio for your guest on an R (3).

❑ **7.** Edit your audio first.

❑ **8.** Delete all audio before the point where you say your countdown to the episode beginning. To use *Onward Nation* as an example, I let our guest know we are about to get started by saying, "Okay, let's get started in 3 . . . 2 . . . 1, Good Morning, *Onward Nation*, I'm Stephen Woessner." This is an audio cue to my guest that we are about to begin the interview. It also serves as an audio cue to my team that any audio (the pre-interview chat) that comes before my "3 . . . 2 . . . 1" can be deleted.

❑ **9.** Delete all audio after you and the guest say good-bye. You do not want any of your post-interview chat accidentally sneaking its way into your episode.

❑ **10.** Apply "Noise Reduction" to your audio—not your guest's. We are still focusing on just your audio for right now.

❑ **11.** Go through and lower the volume on the pieces of audio in between you talking. Be sure to listen to the small audio waves!

❑ **12.** Apply the "DeVerberate" tool to the audio once you have thoroughly gone through the audio and removed any noises you don't want.

❑ **13.** Apply "Match Loudness" so it is -16 db (-3).

❑ **14.** Now you are ready to edit your guest's audio.

❑ **15.** Delete all audio before your guest says, "Thanks, Stephen! Happy to be on *Onward Nation* . . ." As with Step 8, this eliminates any audio from your guest that may have been recorded during your pre-interview chat.

❑ **16.** Delete all audio at the close of the interview. Delete everything after your guest thanks you for being invited onto your show.

❑ **17.** Apply "Noise Reduction" to audio.

❑ **18.** Go through and delete the waves of audio in between the guest talking. Please listen to the audio waves first. They could be important responses to questions you asked during the interview.

❑ **19.** Apply "Match Loudness" so it is -16 db (-3).

❑ **20.** Once you have applied the "Match Loudness" (Match Volume) to your guest's audio, please go to "File" and click on "File" > "New" > "Multitrack Session."

❑ **21.** A window will pop up, and you will want to name the file. We use the file format ON_GuestName_Month(00)_Date(00) (Example: ON_JoeSmith_08_15). We use "ON" to signify *Onward Nation* so we don't get audio files confused with one of the files for a client's podcast.

❑ **22.** Be sure your setting is set to "Podcast." Adobe Audition has a time-saving template specifically designed for podcasters to use when editing audio. Awesome.

❑ **23.** For "Folder Location" please make sure that you click "Browse" and select the folder you created for this episode back in Step 1.

❑ **24.** Click "Okay" and set up your "Multitrack" session.

❑ **25.** Place your audio file in as "Host."

❑ **26.** Place your guest's audio in the "Interview."

❑ **27.** Place your intro audio into "Sound FX."

❑ **28.** Turn off the "Track Effects" for Host, Interview, and Master in the "Track Effects" section to the left of the panel.

❑ **29.** Make sure that in your "Files" section on the left of your panel, you have your audio intro, audio outro, R, L, .mov, and .sesx files together.

❑ **30.** When you start editing on the timeline in your Multitrack session, please be sure that your audio number is first. Cut it (Command K) it from the audio and separate it.

❑ **31.** In the Sound FX, have your intro align with the ending of your audio number.

❑ **32.** Align your guest's audio with your audio—it fits together like a puzzle piece.

❑ **33.** Keeping everything aligned, cut the audio in between pauses of conversation, and bring them closer together. Apply this through-out the entire interview.

❑ **34.** Once you have gone through the entire interview, go back and listen to the full episode. This is a crucial quality-control step to ensure that you catch any audio problems that may have been missed in earlier editing. You can listen to the audio at +65 percent speed to save time.

> ▸ To adjust the playback speed, go to the area above your "Host" audio and click on "Toggle Global Clip Stretching" to be sure

it is activated. It looks like an alarm clock with an arrow underneath. Once you see that it is blue, click "Command A" in your Multitrack, and all of your audio should look bright green.

▶ If all of your audio in your Multitrack is bright green, then go to the top left of your "Host" file and click on the white triangle you see in the corner and drag it toward the middle. Your audio should be squeezed together at this point and a percentage should be displayed.

▶ Once you see that it's at 65 percent, stop, and take a listen to the audio. It should take you a minimum of thirty minutes to listen to the audio if the full episode plays at normal speed in around sixty minutes.

❑ 35. After you have listened to the audio, and made any fixes necessary, add the outro at the end.

❑ 36. Once you have added your audio outro, go up to "Multitrack" > "Mixdown Session to New File" > "Entire Session."

❑ 37. You should now see the audio look completely even all the way through.

❑ 38. Once you have completed the "Mixdown" for your session, go to "File" > "Export" > "File."

❑ 39. When you export your file, the file name should read "ON_Guest-Name_Month(00)_Date(00) Mixdown 1.mp3." Be sure to delete the "Mixdown 1" from the file name to keep things clean. If one of your listeners downloads your full episode from your Smart Podcast Player on your website, the "Mixdown 1" will be the file name they receive unless you delete it.

❑ 40. Your final name should be similar to this: ON_GuestName_Month(00)_Date(00).mp3.

❑ **41.** Then click "Export" and upload it to Google Drive, Dropbox, or your external hard drive for storage. The episode is now ready for uploading into Libsyn.

This wraps up the production-related stages. We recommend getting ten fully edited episodes loaded into Libsyn before launching a one-day-per-week podcast—and twenty-five episodes before launching a daily podcast. The inventory will protect you in case you need to travel for a client, get sick, or want to take a vacation. Otherwise, you may find yourself scrambling to get an episode done that needs to air the next day.

You are now ready to launch your podcast.

CHAPTER 14

STAGE 7:
LAUNCH STRATEGY:
HOW TO REACH THE TOP OF ITUNES

Congratulations on completing the production of your very own Profitable Podcast. The launch recipe in this chapter will provide you with the tactical ingredients to get your podcast to the top of iTunes' New and Noteworthy category. New and Noteworthy is the section of iTunes reserved for podcasts launched during the most recent eight-week time period. When a podcast's eight weeks of New and Noteworthy eligibility expires, iTunes will relocate it to its "What's Hot" category along with all of the other popular top-rated podcasts.

This chapter will help you boost your iTunes rankings, because at the time of this writing, iTunes is still the market leader for podcast distribution. However, the market continues to change as iHeartRadio, Spotify, Google Play, and others become players. In my opinion, the podcast distribution market is ripe for disruption, consolidation, or new advancements in how content is curated for listeners.

Until that time comes, we will focus on iTunes.

Our team has run point on dozens and dozens of podcast launches for our clients. And that experience has time and time again dispelled the myth that a podcast needs to have tens of thousands of downloads, or even thousands of downloads, in order to dominate iTunes' New and Noteworthy rankings. In fact, we have seen podcasts with fewer than 200 downloads per day become number-one-ranked shows in iTunes. You simply need to execute well as it relates to iTunes' vital metrics:

- High-quality audio for your episodes
- Ratings and reviews
- Daily downloads

Your audio quality will be high if you follow the editing recipe shared in the previous chapters. And if you consistently direct your audience to listen to and download your episodes from iTunes, you should be all set with this vital metric, as well.

But it has been our experience that getting ratings and reviews for your show is not as straightforward as it seems. For example, through our research, we have seen that fifty ratings and reviews seems to be the "magic" number to secure a number one ranking in iTunes. However, if your show were to collect fifty ratings and reviews over a six-week period versus fifty ratings and reviews in the first forty-eight hours of launch, that would be a big difference: iTunes will rank the forty-eight-hour podcast much higher and likely award it a number one ranking.

So, part of the ratings and reviews recipe is with what time period you compress your ratings and reviews. The best way to capitalize on this vital metric is by making a list of fifty to seventy people who you know will listen to your show and then give you a rating and review—and ask them to do it between X day and Y day so you can take advantage of the compression.

In addition, our team has a theory that the social footprint of the person who writes a review for your show matters to the iTunes algorithm. So if one of your guests writes a review that's perceived to be high quality, you get points. On the other hand, if you pay a freelancer through Fiverr to boost your rating and reviews, iTunes will recognize the poor quality, and you will not receive the benefit. Thus, be sure to ask for ratings and reviews from credible sources.

Ingredient #1: Register your podcast with iTunes, Stitcher, and Google Play

Earlier, we covered how iTunes and the other platforms are able to access your audio from Libsyn and the RSS feed Libsyn provides you. Now that you are ready to launch, it's time to give iTunes your RSS feed. But please know, once you do so, any and all episodes you have published in Libsyn will become available in iTunes as soon as your podcast has been approved. So it is very important not to provide iTunes with your RSS feed, and not to publish episodes in Libsyn until you are 100 percent ready to go live.

The sign-up processes for iTunes, Stitcher, and Google Play continue to evolve and get better. Consequently, we know that the step-by-step process as it exists today will be obsolete by the time this book makes its way to you. So my team and I created a three-part tutorial video series that we update each time the process changes. You can find the free video series at:

1. PredictiveROI.com/Resource/iTunes-Setup
2. PredictiveROI.com/Resources/Stitcher-Setup
3. PredictiveROI.com/Resources/Google-Play-Setup

Ingredient #2: "Your Interview Is LIVE!" Email to Guests

You or your team should send an email like the following to each guest on the morning their interview goes live so they will know when and how to promote their episodes. Please note: The bracketed sections of the template indicate the content areas you will need to customize for your podcast.

Subject Line: Your Interview Is LIVE!

~Contact.FirstName~

Your interview is LIVE!

You really rocked the interview. I am grateful. Thank you so much!

I would be honored if you would share our interview with your audience!
Some easy ways to do that are to share the links below:

[YourPodcast.com]: Click Here

iTunes: Click Here

Stitcher: Click Here

Google Play: Click Here

Be sure to check out your Show Notes page as [Your Podcast] listeners will
be posting comments—and please feel free to jump into the conversation.

Sincerely Yours,
[Your Name]
[Host of Your Podcast]
[CEO of Your Company]

Ingredient #3: Rate and Review Request Email

I recommend that you and your team send an email similar to the following to
your full email list about two weeks after your show launches. The email provides
your audience with the step-by-step process for giving your show a rating and
writing a review on your behalf. We created this template, and use it for all of our
clients during launch, because the process of rating and reviewing on iTunes can
be confusing. Your audience is doing you a big favor, so you want to make it as
easy as possible for them.

Subject: I need your help

Good Morning [First Name],

Thank you so much for listening to my new podcast, [Name of Podcast].

The response over the last few weeks has been nothing short of incredible.

I am writing today to ask for your help in getting the podcast to the top of the iTunes charts so others can learn lessons from my guests, some of the world's most successful entrepreneurs, leaders, and achievers who are operating at the top of their game.

[Name of Podcast] has quickly become a community of leaders, but I need your help in helping that community to grow.

To get [Name of Podcast] to the top of the iTunes charts, we need to get as many reviews as possible.

Would you please do me a favor and leave a review?

The process is quick and simple. Please go to [this link] and click the blue button that reads "View in iTunes."

Next, click on the link titled "Ratings and Reviews."

Next, click on "Write a Review."

If you are not signed in to iTunes, you will be asked to sign in. If you are already signed in to iTunes, it is likely that you will skip this step.

Finally, you will be able to leave a review. Don't forget the star rating!

I really appreciate your help with this!

Sincerely,
[Your Name]

FIGURE 14-1

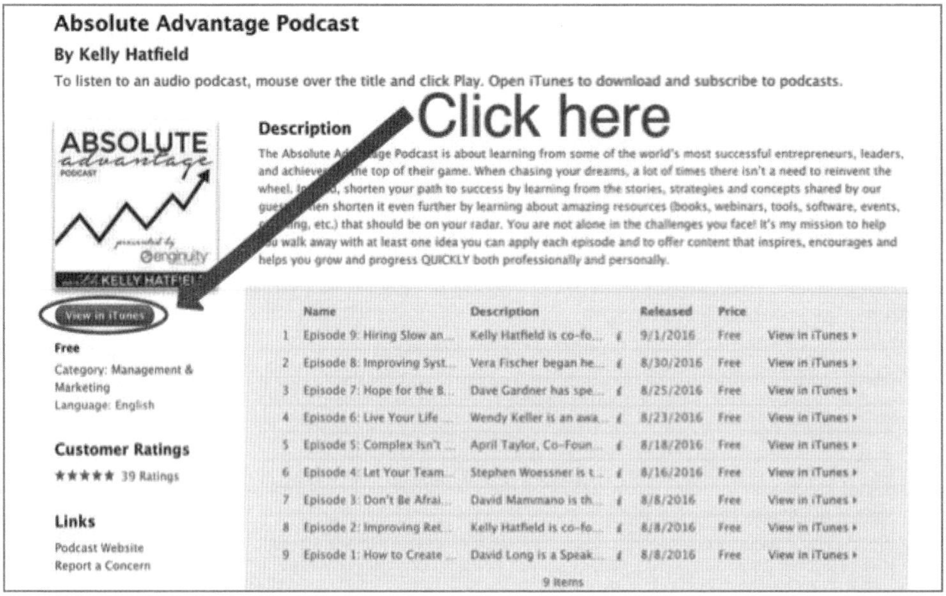

FIGURE 14-2

FIGURE 14-3

FIGURE 14-4

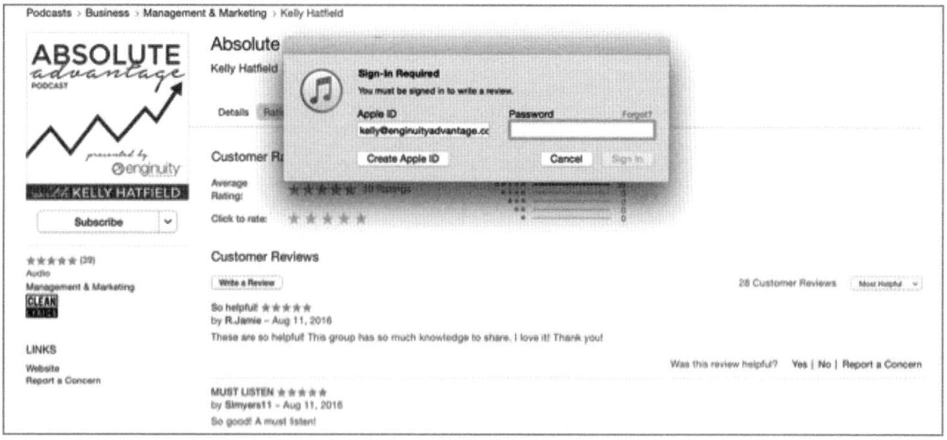

FIGURE 14-5

Figures 14-1, 14-2, 14-3, 14-4, and 14-5 depict the steps for writing a review in iTunes.

I want to share a final thought for you to consider as part of your launch.

Should you spend money on Google AdWords or Facebook campaigns to announce the launch of your podcast? Although tempting to consider—and I encourage you to test paid ads during your launch—the campaigns we have tested in the past did not result in measurable increases to daily downloads.

However, we have had great success in paid Facebook campaigns offering a screaming cool value exchange with email address opt-in. This is an excellent strategy for building your email list, and once you have the subscriber's email address, you can promote your show via email for much less cost and with greater benefit.

I wish you the best of success with your launch!

CHAPTER 15

HOW TO BE
AN EXCELLENT HOST

By the time this book goes to press, *Onward Nation* will have aired nearly 600 episodes. In the process, we have had the incredible opportunity to learn directly from today's top business owners. The depth of knowledge, wisdom, and expertise generously shared by our guests never ceases to amaze me. They freely take us inside their businesses, their hopes, their dreams, their aspirations, their failures, and then weave it all together in this wonderful, beautiful tapestry that we call an episode.

My vital priority during these conversations is not to get in the way of my guests doing what they are there to do. I learned early on that the show is not at all about me. Our guests are the stars, and when the host can demonstrate that fact throughout the conversation, the result will be an epic interview.

This chapter will serve as your practical guide to becoming an excellent host. I will share several of my insights that I have learned along the way as well as what I learned from two *Onward Nation* guests and fellow podcasters: Drew McLellan and John Livesay.

Drew McLellan, top dog at the Agency Management Institute, is the host of the brilliant podcast *Build a Better Agency*. Drew has owned and operated his own agency for the past twenty years. He also works with more than 250 small to midsize agencies a year in a variety of ways: peer network groups, workshops for owners and their leadership teams, on-site consulting, and one-to-one coaching with owners.

John Livesay is the host of the successful podcast *The Successful Pitch. Inc.* magazine calls John the "Pitch Whisperer." He is the author of the book also entitled *The Successful Pitch*. John helps CEOs craft a compelling pitch to investors in a way that inspires them to join a start-up's team. Also, John and Judy Robinett are business partners in *Crack the Funding Code*, a webinar/workbook that gets founders funded fast.

Let's get started.

In fiction, a "foil" is a character who contrasts with another character (usually the protagonist) in order to highlight particular qualities of the other character. In my opinion, your ability to play the role of the foil will determine whether you are an excellent or a mediocre host. You need to use your podcast to help your guests advance their agendas by sharing *their* wisdom and expertise—not yours.

Avoid telling stories about yourself even if they support what your guest just said. Your role is not to validate what your guest just said. Your guests don't need you to validate their experience. Attempting to do so can be seen as arrogant; it could look like you're trying to steal the show. Don't do that. Instead, summarize, reflect back to your guests the impactful highlights of what they have just shared, add a comment or two from what you have seen in your experience, and then ask your guest if you got all of that correct.

By asking the question, "Did I get all of that correct, Sally?" you do three things:

- Demonstrate to Sally that you are listening to every word she shares
- Show that what she said mattered because you connected it to your own experience
- Prompt Sally to go deeper with her examples and experience sharing

Start out the conversation with some light questions; build trust and rapport in the first few minutes. Be engaging, be personable, and if you are able to make your guest laugh in the first couple of minutes, congratulations—you're building rapport. Avoid asking deep, emotionally charged questions early on in the interview. It will not go well. Your guest will likely think you are trying to move too deep too quickly.

I asked Drew McLellan for his insights on the most critical things business owners need to master to be successful at podcasting. Drew shared that he believes it is a combination of skills, the most important of which is for the host to check their ego at the door. "My job when I'm hosting is to augment and put the spotlight on my guest and their expertise," Drew said. "I do that by listening really hard to what they say and running it through my filter of, 'What else would an agency owner want to know about that?' I'm not talking over them, I'm not trying to jump in and show how much I know about the topic. I am listening super hard. I am asking what I hope are great follow-up questions. I'm really trying to stay out of the guest's way so they have as much airtime as possible to share their expertise.

"I think part of listening with real intent is to be able to ask the question that I'm always thinking, 'If somebody is driving while they're listening to this, or walking on the treadmill, or whatever, what would they want me to ask?' Or, do I frustrate them by not asking the follow-up questions that they want me to ask? I'm always listening with that intent. 'What should I be asking next? What did somebody want to hear more about or how would they want to drill deeper into this?' I'm trying to ask those questions because I don't want any of my listeners thinking, 'I can't believe he didn't ask X!'"

I also asked John Livesay for his insights on critical skills. He explained to me why and how he uses empathy and listening to make connections with guests. "One of the investors on my show told me that the more empathy you show for your customer, the more the customer feels like you understand that customer and can solve that problem," John said. "I think what makes you have empathy for someone is your ability to listen to them and put yourself in their shoes. The more you can do that with your guests and respond to what they're saying and make them feel heard and then summarize what you're hearing for your audience as the takeaways, that, in my opinion, is what it takes to be really great as a podcast host."

One of the best ways to ensure your excellence as a host is in how you help a guest prepare to be a great guest on your show. You can do that by implementing the Guest Advocacy System illustrated earlier in this book. You ought to supplement this system by personally setting expectations with guests. In my opinion, Drew does this masterfully well. Drew shared with me, "What I discovered is, that the minute I checked my ego at the door, I realized the show wasn't about somebody listening to me, it was about me cultivating this great list of guests and serving guests well, which serves my audience well. So if I allow my guests to have the spotlight, and I allow them to really share their expertise, and I prep them properly, so it's like, 'Look, there is no selling, this is not about you getting clients, this is about you generously sharing your expertise. Here are the kind of questions I'm going to ask; if you're not comfortable answering those questions, don't come on the show.' None of that was about me. It's about serving up the best content possible for my audience by putting my guest in the best possible light."

✓ CHECKLIST FOR HOSTING WITH EXCELLENCE ✓

❑ Check your ego at the door. Your show is about making your guest the star. Your show should not be about you.

❑ Study. Listen to other hosts and hear how they interact with their guests.

❑ Keep the conversation casual yet focused on the results you want to deliver to your audience.

❑ Help your guests prepare by implementing a Guest Advocacy System so they receive email and text reminders before your interview as well as tips on how to sound their best during the recording.

❑ Also help your guests prepare by emailing them your questions in advance along with some insights regarding your audience so your guests have context and know how best to answer your questions.

❑ Begin on time and end on time. This shows respect for your guest's schedule.

❑ Turn off your email, your cell phone, and all social media, and listen intently to your guest so you can think of follow-up questions your audience would want you to ask.

❑ Summarize and recap your guest's awesomeness during the interview. Then ask your guest if you got the summary right or if you've missed something. This is the perfect invitation to a guest to go deeper and share even more value with your audience.

❑ Thank the guest before the interview, during the interview, and after the interview for taking the time to generously share their wisdom with your audience.

❑ Have confidence. You are good enough to do this. You are worthy. You will make a difference in the world by sharing the wisdom of your guests. You are building a nation of true fans. Kick the impostor syndrome to the curb by remembering the wise words of Walter D. Wintle, quoted by Napoleon Hill, author of *Think and Grow Rich*:

> If you think you are beaten, you are,
> If you think you dare not, you don't.
> If you like to win, but you think you can't,
> It is almost certain you won't.
>
> If you think you'll lose, you're lost,
> For out of the world we find,
> Success begins with a person's will—
> It's all in the state of mind.
>
> If you think you're outclassed, you are,
> You've got to think high to rise,
> You've got to be sure of yourself before
> You can ever win a prize.
>
> Life's battles don't always go
> To the stronger or faster man
> But soon or late the one who wins
> Is the one WHO THINKS HE CAN!
>
> —WALTER D. WINTLE

CHAPTER 16

HOW TO ATTRACT SPONSORSHIPS

Interview with Linda Hollander

learned everything I know about the *ins and outs* of sponsor strategy—or the best practices for properly positioning a podcast so it can be sold to a top-tier corporate sponsor—by interviewing Linda Hollander, one of today's leading authorities on the topic of sponsorships. Both *Inc.* magazine and *Entrepreneur* magazine have featured Linda as the industry leader in how to sell corporate sponsorships. Linda has more than twenty years of experience as a business owner. Her clients and sponsors include Microsoft, FedEx, Citibank, Mattel, Bank of America, Marriott, Health Net, American Airlines, IBM, and Walmart. Her client list reads like a "Who's Who" in corporate sponsorship. You can find Linda at www.sponsorconcierge.com.

This chapter distills the Q&A between Linda Hollander and me. I wanted you to read in Linda's own words how she became today's leading authority in sponsorships. Her story is compelling because she did it even though she was starting at zero.

You can do the same if you follow the master blueprint she provides in this chapter.

Q: Linda, take us back to the beginning and your first event so business owners reading this can have the full context of what you have accomplished.

Linda: I've had the privilege of working with some great "Top Tier" sponsors but it wasn't always that way. Many of our clients early on in our business were women so I wanted to start the *Women's Small Business Expo* to deliver even more value to our clients. But I needed sponsors because putting on an event is cash intensive. Ultimately, my first sponsors were Bank of America, Walmart, and IBM.

I had never done an event in my life. I had no idea how to do an event. I had no experience. I had no following. I had my parents on my email list. I put my brother-in-law on my email list. They weren't going to tell me *no*. If I could have put my cat on there, I would have. But despite how I started out, I was able to attract several top-tier sponsors.

And when our event attendees came, they would ask me, "How the heck are you getting these sponsors? I thought you had to be a big company and have all this experience and track record," and I said, "Absolutely no." Then I knew there was a need in the marketplace for training business owners on how to attract sponsors.

I lost a lot of time and money when I started to learn the sponsorship game. It took me six months to get my first proposal together. I lost $75,000 in the process. It was painful; it was excruciating. Some people wouldn't even talk to me because I was a micro-business. But, there were also people who said, "You know what? I'll talk to you. I'll help you." Then I said to myself, "When I learn this stuff, I'm going to teach other business owners how to do it."

Q: Let's start off with some definitions. When we hear "sponsor," that could mean different things depending upon someone's business model. What does sponsorship mean, what does a sponsor want to sponsor, are they programs, events, or businesses?

Linda: The definition of sponsorship is "*Connecting a company with people who can buy things.*" If you know people who can buy stuff, then you can get sponsors. It is a lot simpler than what most business owners think.

If you have a business—that could be sponsored. If you host a radio show, or a podcast, or a television show, YouTube show, or a blog—all of that can be sponsored. Of course, if you do an event you can get sponsors because sponsors love events.

If you're a speaker or an author, you can get sponsored, because as a speaker and an author you have access to an audience—a fan base of people—who know your work and know your book, and as a speaker you command the platform. Companies don't have people who can speak, who can command a platform, or capture the attention of an audience.

Q: What are some of the biggest mistakes you see business owners making time and time again as they pursue sponsorships?

Linda: There are a few mistakes, and I've made all of them, so I can share from experience. The first mistake, believe it or not, is not asking for enough money.

Asking for too little money can hurt a business owner because they are, in effect, telling a sponsor they don't have anything of value to offer. I often get calls from business owners who are trying to sell their $500 sponsor package. They're going to be presenting to a busy, stressed-out person inside a company, who, if they see a sponsor package priced at $500, they're going to think the business owner doesn't have anything of value.

In the sponsorship process, you have what's called your "Champion," and this is the person in the sponsoring company who loves you, but they have to sell you and your program to their colleagues, their team, and their boss, and maybe the people working under them to get it approved. Your pricing strategy needs to communicate value in order for them to do that. For most of our clients, what we see them typically get is between $10,000 and $100,000 in annual sponsor fees.

If you do an event, if you have a podcast, or something else that is episode-to-episode, bundle everything together for the year and sell an annual sponsorship because you're going to be more successful in properly positioning yourself with sponsors.

The second mistake business owners make is not using an industry standard proposal.

Your sponsor proposal is one of the most important but least understood documents. You have to use an industry standard format or you will not get funded. Your proposal must look amazing and have the right compelling benefits. The two biggest mistakes are asking for too little money and not having a good proposal.

Q: Let's say you're a podcaster. Sounds like you would try to sell an annual sponsorship of your show instead of weekly episodes, but you would also package in your entire platform including social media, email lists, webinars, events, etc., right?

Linda: Yes, you want them to sponsor your entire brand—not a single show. It took me a while to figure this out, because at first I started to have sponsors for my events and then I thought, "Wait a minute, I've got a whole brand here." When I had them sponsor my brand, I made a whole lot more money. Instead of a business owner saying, "I'm a podcaster," you should brand yourself as a "media company" who does podcasting because sponsors are not quite in love with podcasting yet. It's still new. It's still cutting edge. But if you say you're a media company, then their ears are going to perk up. Then they're going to be interested.

Talk about your podcast, but then talk about the other things you do, such as email blasts, social media, maybe even YouTube, etc. Talk about all of the touch points you have. Let's go back to the definition of sponsorship: "*Connecting a company to people who buy things*." Tell them how you can connect them to people who could buy their stuff.

Q: Do I diminish my own brand if I go get a sponsor?

Linda: I'm asked that question a lot, because as business owners, we want to be independent, we don't want to have a company influence what we're going to say, and we don't want the appearance that we're biased. I have never had a sponsor try to influence my content in sixteen years of doing this. And if they ever did, I would just say, "Hey, that's not part of the program." You design your program—the sponsor writes the check—that's what goes on with sponsorships.

Also, the promotion of your sponsor does not have to be outlandish or in your face. The promotion can be elegant and understated, such as signage, banner ads, or things you put on your website. And if you do recommend a company like when I was working with, let's say, Citibank, and I would recommend Citibank, then I disclosed it by saying, "I need to disclose that Citibank is my sponsor," and then you are in integrity by disclosing it.

Q: Are there any secrets to success business owners need to apply in order to be successful in attracting a sponsor?

Linda: It would be to make the sponsor the star. Most business owners when they try to get a sponsor, they fall into the trap of talking about what their business does; they might say things like, "I have this great podcast, I have this great book, I have a great business, I have a great nonprofit, or event, etc." Business owners can sometimes talk about themselves and that's not the way to get a sponsor.

The way to get a sponsor is to talk to the sponsor about what you can do for them. Say, "Hey, Mr., Ms. Sponsor, I'm going to educate people about your products and your services. I'm going to help you increase your product and your brand loyalty. I'm going to help you grow your customer base. I'm going to help you drive sales and traffic."

Do you see the difference?

You're saying, "Hey, the sponsor is the star," and your prospective sponsor is going to look at that and say, "Hey, this business owner understands that it's about me and not about them." You'll tell them a little bit about what you do because they have to understand it, but mostly what you're going to tell the sponsor is, "Here's how I'm going to benefit your company; here's what I'm going to do for you."

Q: Let's talk timelines. How fast does, or maybe how long is, the sales cycle you typically see for attracting $10,000 to $100,000 sponsorships?

Linda: Sponsorships are a relationship business. You need time to develop relationships with companies. Here's where it's going to be maybe a little bit of a shock to business owners. I recommend eight months to a year before you need the funding to start approaching prospective sponsors. Let me tell you why. If you're approaching Microsoft, FedEx, Staples (those are called the "Top Tier" sponsors), they have a process. You have to apply and you have to wait for them to approve it. They like to have a lot of lead time because whatever you are doing you have to talk about how you are going to work with their company, what kind of a program you are going to build together, and it takes time to develop that depth of relationship.

It will take time to get your first sponsor. Now, let me tell you how you could do it quicker. There are "Top Tier" sponsors and then there are "Second Tier" sponsors. In the banking industry (and banks are a great place to go to get sponsorship) I've worked with Bank of America and I've worked with Citibank. They are Top Tier. But there may be a local community bank where you live. There may be an up-and-coming player in the banking industry you might want to work with. That won't take as long because it's easier to get to the decision-makers and to get that process of sponsorship started.

The amazing thing about sponsorship being a relationship business is that there is something called renewals in sponsorship. And renewals are magic. Renewals are your cash machine, because if a sponsor likes you, they can fund you this year, next year, and the next year. I've sold multiyear sponsorships with FedEx and Citibank. My clients have had multiyear contracts with Verizon, Dole Foods, and Black and Decker just to name a few.

It's not a quick-cash strategy. It is a long-term strategy to fund your business.

That's why we tell business owners to go for a one-year contract because one year is about enough time to really analyze the relationship and if the sponsor wants to continue. If your sponsorship is from event-to-event, or episode-to-episode, a sponsor is not going to see that much growth as far as return on investment, so they are less likely to renew.

Q: Let's get tactical and think about key steps in the process, the action plan, things that are going to improve the probability of success. If you were to give business owners one, two, or three things they need to do, what would those steps be?

Linda: I'm going to share a three-step process to attracting a sponsor.

The first part is to do what we call the "Sponsor Wish List." The wish list is the list of companies that you would like to have as sponsors. Remember in your sponsor wish list to include both Top Tier and the Second Tier sponsors. Most business owners when they start their wish list think only of Top Tier sponsors. Go deeper. We've already talked about the banking industry, so let's talk insurance. I know I'm talking about boring companies like banking and insurance when most business owners want glam sponsors like fashion, cosmetics, and accessories. But the boring companies have the money.

Let's take the insurance category, you're going to think of State Farm, and Aflac, and all the ones that have paid to be top of mind. Then go a little deeper by doing some Google searches into smaller insurance companies, the up-and-coming brands, because the up-and-coming brands need you to get their name out. They don't have the brand awareness of the big brands.

I'll give you an example of that. I worked with a company called Evolution Insurance Brokers. Nobody has ever heard of Evolution Insurance Brokers, and that is exactly why they sponsored me. They wanted to get the word out about their company. They're not Aflac, they're not State Farm, they're not the big players in the industry.

The Second Tiers have money to invest. I can't disclose exactly the value of the sponsorship, but it was five figures.

Step two is preparing your professional proposal. You want to write that industry-standard sponsor proposal.

The full sponsor proposal is about eight to ten pages in length, and here's what it includes:

- A description of your "property." Write down the word property because what you do now is called the "property." Your podcast is a property. Your book is a property. Your speaking business is a property. Your business, your event, your nonprofit, whatever you are doing is called a property. You want to describe that.

- You should include your sponsor's goals, which should be similar to what we talked about earlier in this chapter, such as increasing brand loyalty and customer base, educating people, and driving traffic and sales, and all that.

- You should include a one-page marketing plan. It includes all the ways you're going to get the word out about the sponsor. Sponsors are interested in this because marketing is the difference between a good idea someone has in their head and something that actually has legs and is sustainable.

- You should include your demographics. Whether your demographics are mothers, the parent market, the entrepreneurial market, the urban youth, the baby boomer market, you need to describe your demographics. Include any testimonials you have.

- You should include your sponsor fees like the ones we've talked about.

- The last thing, and here is how we write proposals differently from anyone else in the country, is storytelling.

You want to have good storytelling inside your proposal. We call it "passion points" in the sponsor industry. I've sold sponsors because I didn't just put in the proposal what's called your "pretty bio." The pretty bio is your education, and the awards you won, and your experience. All of that is nice but what you want is to be vulnerable; you need to make a human connection, because you're not just pitching to a faceless cooperation. You are pitching to a person, a human being, and you want to show your humanity.

In my story, I talk about how I was in the poverty trap. I talk about how I was in an abusive relationship. My story has helped me secure sponsors because you want them to see you as a real person. The emotional connection is so important. You want to put beautiful storytelling in there. If you don't want to include your own story, put the story of someone you've helped through the work you do.

Be sure to include some emotion. Business owners often make the mistake of thinking, "Oh, I'm going to impress them, and I'm going to put facts, and figures, and statistics in there." But unfortunately, that is not going to help you rise above the competition. Be human.

Q: Are there any other tools, any other resources you think business owners ought to study to make this process as efficient and effective as possible?

Linda: My website is www.sponsorconcierge.com, and there are two free gifts. One is the "Number 1 Secret to Getting Corporate Sponsors." And the second is that I do free sponsor strategy sessions with business owners so they can book a sponsor strategy session with me, and I will take a look at what they are currently doing, and together, we will develop a success strategy to get them sponsors.

Q: Any final advice you want to share or anything you think we might have missed?

Linda: I want business owners to know they can do this. The number one question I am asked is, "Why would a sponsor want to work with little ol' me? I'm just getting started. I'm not a big company. I don't have a track record. I don't have a big following." Please know you can do this. You have value. You have things a sponsor is going to be attracted to. You just need to package it in the right way.

Here's a quick story about how I got a sponsor. I live in Los Angeles, California, so when I first had the idea to do my initial event, I was driving around in my clunker car, and I'm of course stuck in a traffic jam. I look up and see a billboard for Bank of America and there's a woman featured within the billboard design, so I think to myself, "Okay, they're trying to get the women's market."

Immediately, I start doing self-sabotaging and thinking, "Why the heck would they talk to me? I'm just working from my home from my kitchen table. I'm not a big company. What the heck am I going to offer Bank of America?"

But my dream and mission to help people was so strong that I couldn't get it out of my head. So I got the courage to make a call to Bank of America and finally got the person who could green-light the sponsorships. I finished my proposal, got everything done, and had an appointment at their office. Thank goodness there was a desk between him and me because my knees were knocking.

Then he said to me, "Well, let's see your proposal," and I handed it to him. And he said, "Okay, well we're going to go for this level of sponsorship," and it was a five-figure sponsorship. I had to act like I did this all the time so I said, "Oh, great," and I had to shake his hand, but my hand was so clammy I had to wipe it off!

I got back in my car and did the happy dance right there in the parking lot! I drove home, and I waved to all the Bank of America branches on my way home.

You never know what's going to happen. It all starts with a thought. It starts with a dream. It starts with a vision. We're taught to have these big dreams but we're not taught how to finance the dreams, and dreams take money, and that's where sponsors come in.

You can do this! Hold your head up high. Know that you have quality and you bring value to your sponsors, and—you can fund your dreams.

CHAPTER 17

GETTING IT ALL DONE: RECRUIT ROCK STAR UNPAID INTERNS

You will need a team of highly productive people working alongside you to help create and launch your profitable podcast. But this doesn't mean you have to hire several full-time employees or virtual assistants. Instead, I recommend that you consider recruiting and hiring a team of A Players who are not paid members of your team, but unpaid interns. Yes, I did just recommend unpaid interns.

At Predictive ROI, we have built an outstanding internship program that has provided twenty-four unpaid internships to students in their senior year of study at Duke University, Purdue University, The Ohio State University, University of Northern Iowa, University of Wisconsin–La Crosse, and other universities throughout the country.

I decided to include this chapter on how to recruit rock star interns for a couple of reasons:

- Business owners tend not to have a process in place for recruiting rock star interns. They often recruit interns who are not motivated, who are looking to augment their résumés, and who did just the bare minimum during the semester. These are not the high performers you need on your team—or the type of interns you will recruit if you follow this recipe.
- Because of the less-than-stellar performance from past interns, business owners either abandon their internship programs, or they come to believe that it is unrealistic to recruit a team of unpaid interns. This is a myth. Two years ago, we recruited a team of six unpaid interns to work on a specific social media lead gen project. Katherine Bartlett on my team managed the day-to-day activity of each of the six interns. Katherine, at the time, was also an intern. She is now a member of my leadership team at Predictive ROI, where she oversees all of our agency's content development.

Our recipe for recruiting rock star interns is exceptional. I am going to share all of the ingredients so you can implement it into your business right away.

But before I do, I want you to meet several rock stars from our Predictive ROI team who pull the levers to the day-to-day production behind *Onward Nation*.

Let me first share more about Katherine. She is the wizard behind all of our episodes—how they sound and how they look on social media. Katherine has grown so much over the last several years that she is now our vice president of content marketing at Predictive ROI and now leads our team of content development experts. Any content produced for Predictive ROI clients is the result of Katherine and her team.

We knew we had a high performer on our hands with Katherine because she is one of those people who raises her hand and says—"Um, I know that I am only required to do ten hours per week for this internship. But, could I do more?"

Our response was, "Oh my. Yes, please!"

When her internship was complete, we transitioned Katherine to what we call a "Super Intern" while she finished her final semester at the University of Northern Iowa. She received a small financial stipend while she focused on her remaining education. And when she graduated, she became a full-time member of our team. Katherine is a rock star.

Then there is Louie Schuth. Louie is our rock star in charge of writing all our Show Notes, creating and sending email campaigns, writing blog posts, implementing our Twitter strategy, and posting our LinkedIn articles.

We are thrilled to have Louie as a member of our team because he and Katherine are cut from the same "Can I do more?" cloth.

We started Louie with a variety of writing projects and he quickly excelled. He then asked if he could allocate a portion of his time to WordPress and managing some of our websites. We said, "Um, yes please!"

No surprise—Louie excelled there, too.

He is the one who stays up late with me Tuesday nights before each solocast airs the next day to make sure the Show Notes and audio file are set correctly.

An amazing writer and a graduate of the University of Wisconsin–La Crosse, Louie finished his internship and is now a full-time member of our team just like Katherine. We have big plans for Louie.

Then there is Jessica Zickert, who, at the time of this writing, is finishing her final semester at the University of Wisconsin–La Crosse. Jessica is part of Katherine's content marketing team and has been successfully mentored through our production process. Jessica is such a rock star that she has assumed the day-to-day editing of *Onward Nation* episodes from Katherine. She has followed Kat's recipe flawlessly.

Jessica's level of proactivity is also off the charts. For example, when I make a mistake while recording an interview with a guest, I try to immediately loop back to Jessica to let her know so she can try to clean up my mistake in post-production editing. But, when I did that recently, she let me know that she had already found my mistake and corrected it. Bam! That's proactive.

Last but not least, I'd like to introduce you to Erik Jensen, our vice president of client services at Predictive ROI. Erik, who is also a member of both our leadership and ownership teams, oversees all of our operations.

I met Erik while I was serving as a member of the academic staff at the University of Wisconsin–La Crosse. One day, the chair of our marketing department in the College of Business suggested to Erik that he should come see me regarding a business plan he and his business partner were developing for a competition at Duke University. We met, and I was blown away by Erik's professionalism. Later that night, I said to my wife, "Wow, this guy is amazing. He and I are going to work together on something someday."

Several years later, Erik became our first intern at Predictive ROI. Later, he joined our team as full-time employee number three with the title of "Associate." In less than a year, we promoted Erik to engagement manager, then to our leadership team, and then to vice president of client services.

Erik is a rock star in the truest sense. He helped set the standard by which we evaluate and measure all interns. He invested a full-time schedule toward his internship even though it wasn't required. That's the type of heart you are looking for in your interns, too.

Create a demanding internship program. Treat your unpaid interns exactly the way you treat your full-time members. Tell your candidates they are interviewing for the "Marine Corps of Internships," and you will get a higher level of production and proactivity.

Here's our recipe.

First, we accept only students in their senior year of school. While we have had positive experiences with juniors and graduates, too, we decided to recruit only seniors going forward because we found them to be the most motivated, eager to learn, and hungry to gain experience. After all, graduation is looming and so are their job searches.

Ingredient #1

Define your culture with your leadership team and employees and post a page on your website for candidates to study.

On our culture page for Predictive ROI, we define with the following phrases (and more):

We promise to provide our clients with the very best, most outstanding consulting and training services available.

We are so committed to being outstanding that we deliver a minimum of 200 percent financial return on investment to clients. We take it further by guaranteeing each client's ROI.

And refund our fee if we do not deliver what we promise.

We demand a standard of excellence of ourselves and are committed to delivering that standard to clients 100 percent of the time. No excuses or exceptions.

We are a team. We work hard. We rise together—because as our clients succeed—we succeed.

You can find our full culture description here: http://predictiveroi.com/culture/.

Ingredient #2

Write a position description that is in line with your culture and post it on your website.

We clearly define who and what we're looking for in our position descriptions. Here's how we begin our description of what we do—and who exactly we are looking for:

Predictive ROI is a growing content marketing and lead gen agency that works with an array of visionary businesses in many industries. We work with our clients to help them achieve explosive growth by reaching their digital goals. This includes increasing their ROI and enhancing their brand across many platforms/mediums. We are looking for candidates who embody our standard of excellence and our culture of teamwork, and who are enthusiastic about learning while delivering their best work. We offer the flexibility of working remotely, a robust on-boarding program, training through our Predictive ROI Institute, a team of like-minded high achievers, and opportunities for advancement.

If you are a member of the Predictive team, or a client, you are family. We work together to achieve our goals; we care, and we go all in to get it done.

You can find full position descriptions here: http://predictiveroi.com/digital-marketing-careers/.

Ingredient #3

Post testimonials/social proof on your website because "A Players" want to work with other "A Players"—or where other "A Players" have worked.

"The team at Predictive ROI is incredible. They are so talented and passionate about this industry, and that really makes such a difference. I feel like I have learned much more through this internship than I ever expected. With every step of the way, I felt involved in the process and that my thoughts and ideas mattered. Through the help of some pretty great mentors, I was able to not only learn more about this industry, but was able to apply what I was learning first-hand."—Whitney Puent

"There's one word that comes to mind when looking to describe the Predictive ROI internship: special. Predictive ROI gives you the opportunity to do great work that has an impact. But, more importantly, at Predictive ROI you work with the greatest team you could ever ask for, a team that will have your back and guide you so that you're better prepared for the working world, and better prepared for life. If you're willing to put in the hard work, don't think twice about applying for an internship with Predictive ROI. You won't regret it."—Louie Schuth

"Applying for an internship with Predictive ROI was the best decision I've made in a long time. Going into my final semester of college, I knew I wanted an internship that would allow me to hone and develop my professional skills by making impactful contributions within an organization. An internship with Predictive ROI gives you exactly that. At Predictive ROI, you are given the opportunity to work with an unbelievable team that will teach you the tools and skills needed to be successful in your career."

—Alex Krupski

Ingredient #4

Weed out B and C Players by sending a prequalifying email with challenging, thought-provoking questions to each candidate.

We send the following email immediately after receiving someone's application/résumé:

[Candidate's First Name], thank you for your interest in our internship!

As the first step in our process, please review the following questions and email us back your thoughts for each.

Your answers to each question will give our team an opportunity to: (1) understand how we can create the right internship experience for you and ensure that you learn everything you want to learn, (2) evaluate your written communication skills, and (3) assess your depth of interest in joining our team.

1. Please introduce yourself (beyond what we can learn by reading your résumé) and discuss why our internship is of interest to you.

2. Please describe the top three things you would like to learn during this internship. We encourage you to be as specific as possible.

3. Tell us about your digital marketing experience up to this point (and if it is zero . . . that is okay).

4. Things we cannot teach are work ethic, commitment to teammates, integrity, and excellence. Please share an example of when you consistently demonstrated excellence in your work.

5. Please share an example of when you demonstrated integrity.

6. What are the attributes or qualities you look for in teammates?

7. How can we help support your growth and development during this internship?

8. This is my direct email address—please feel free to reply here.

We look forward to talking with you.

Please let me know if you have any questions or concerns.

Sincerely Yours,
Stephen Woessner
Host of the Onward Nation podcast
CEO of Predictive ROI

Ingredient #5

Conduct an initial call to assess cultural fit and subject matter expertise deep dive.

If the answers provided back meet our standard of excellence, we schedule a subject matter expertise–focused phone call in order to assess:

- Cultural fit
- Depth of technical/content marketing knowledge

The candidate's current knowledge is not a deal breaker because we train our interns—but it is good to have a baseline. I also make a decision—along with the candidate—on whether or not there is a good enough fit to move on to Ingredient #6.

Ingredient #6

Conduct a team interview with the candidate.

We then schedule and conduct team interviews with candidates. Katherine, Erik, Alex Krupski (also a former intern who is now our full-time search engine optimization and systems specialist), and I conduct each interview. Our aim during this interview is to answer any questions from the candidate about Predictive ROI, the internship, and where the company is headed. We ask a lot of questions about teamwork, proactivity, independent working, and critical thinking. It's important to note that I have one vote of four during the debrief sessions following each interview. Making decisions as a team is part of our culture. So is giving Katherine, Erik, and Alex the same decision-making authority as me during the process. I am a firm believer that they should select their new teammates.

Ingredient #7

Make a go or no-go decision—then send "Congratulations" email.

> Good Morning [Candidate's First Name], thank you again for your time yesterday afternoon!
>
> I am excited to give you a very warm welcome to the Predictive ROI team.
>
> Katherine, Erik, Alex, and I thoroughly enjoyed our time with you yesterday and look forward to having your contribution to the work we are all doing.
>
> I am preparing a formal acceptance letter that will detail initial responsibilities, internship duration, etc. I will email it to you on Friday for your review and approval.
>
> But at this point . . . would Monday be a good start date for you?
>
> And would you be able to attend our 8:45 A.M. kick-start meeting via Zoom?
>
> Onward with gusto!

Ingredient #8

Kick off the semester-long internship.

After the candidate has accepted our internship, we bring her into our daily kick-start meetings every morning at 8:45. We all work on four issues:

1. My three most vital priorities for the day are . . .
2. What I didn't get done yesterday but should have (not a judgment question—but an ask for teamwork)
3. This is where I need some help . . .
4. I do/don't have available time today

Lastly, your probability of creating a solid internship program rests in your willingness to take vital projects off your plate and give them to your interns. I encourage you to put them on the front lines with clients and task them with meaningful work. They will love you for it, and you will continue to recruit *rock star unpaid interns.*

DON'T QUIT—WIN THE OSCAR INSTEAD

Congratulations on making it to the end of this book. I know it wasn't easy.

But now you need to keep building the momentum and launch your own profitable podcast. The only way you can do that is to push yourself to think past the thoughts of quitting that will soon be crashing against you—if they haven't already started. If you are feeling that right now—rest assured—that is the impostor syndrome just trying to steal your destiny from you.

Rather than quitting, my hope for you is that you will win the Oscar instead. I will illustrate the tenacity you need through this lesson I learned from Tony Robbins. It is a story you may already know—a story about grit, perseverance, and about being so committed to what you want to do—what you believe in—that you work desperately to create it.

The story is about Sylvester Stallone—one of Hollywood's most successful actors. But Stallone didn't have success handed to him; he had to earn it. He had to knock down obstacles and barriers to prove he was worthy. He had to starve, he had to endure hardship, he had to freeze in his New York City apartment, he had to go without everything, and he had to find warmth in the public library.

He faced more than 1,500 brutal and cruel rejections from talent scouts and agents. And yet, he did not quit.

Sylvester Stallone had been listening to some of Tony's audio programs and really liked them. So Stallone did what any of us would do—he invited Tony over to dinner so they could talk things over.

Before dinner, Tony said to Stallone, "You know, I have heard your story from other people, but I would really love to hear it from the horse's mouth. I don't know how much is mythology or urban myth or how much is true."

Stallone agreed to share his life story with Tony. He had always known what he wanted to do—ever since he was very young. He wanted to be in the movie business. Period. Not TV, but the movies. Being in the movies was an opportunity to help people escape the realities of their day. But more than that, it was an opportunity to inspire audiences.

Stallone's drive—his passion—is what makes his movies inspiring. He helps audiences see how they could overcome unbelievable obstacles, because in his own life, he feels that he has done that.

For example, Stallone told Tony that when he was born he was pulled out of his mother's womb with forceps. That's why he looks and talks the way he does. With resolve in his voice, he said to Tony, "I really wanted to do this—to be in the movies. I know why I wanted to do it and I wasn't going to settle for anything else."

Stallone went out to try to get acting jobs. But it's not like he went, "Yo, Adrian," and the casting directors said, "Oh, wait, you're a star." In fact, the early years of Stallone's career didn't work out real well. He was alone, hungry, and grinding it out—just to survive.

Casting directors looked at Stallone and said things like, "You're stupid looking; do something else." They made fun of the way Stallone talked, and they told him that there was no place for him in the movies. They said, "You're never going to be a star. You're insane. No one is going to want to listen to someone who looks and sounds dopey, and talks out the side of their mouth." Imagine if someone said that to you. How would you feel? What would you do? Would you quit?

Stallone received no, after no, after no . . . after no. He told Tony that he was thrown out of more than 1,500 agent offices in New York. Tony said, "Hey, wait a minute; there aren't 1,500 agents in New York."

Stallone said, "Yeah, I know . . . I've been to all of them five, six, seven, eight, or nine times."

He then shared with Tony a time he had made it to an agent's office at four in the afternoon and the agent wouldn't agree to see Stallone. Stallone refused to leave. He stayed there all night until the agent came back the next morning.

His persistence paid off. He landed his first movie role. Tony said, "Oh really, I thought *Rocky* was your first movie?" He said this other movie that Tony had never heard of was his first movie. Tony asked him what character he played, and Stallone said, "Oh, well, I was in it for about twenty seconds, and I was a thug that somebody beat up because they made me feel like people hate your guts so you getting beat up will be a good thing."

He did three movies like that but didn't get anything more. Yet, he kept going out to look. He received only rejection, rejection, and more rejection. Did he give up? Did he quit? Heck no!

Finally Stallone realized that it wasn't working. So he changed his approach. He was desperate. He was starving. He couldn't afford to heat his apartment. His wife was screaming at him every day to go get a job.

So Tony asked him, "Well, why didn't you go out and get a job?"

Stallone said, "Because I knew that if I got a job, I would get seduced back, and I would lose my hunger. And the only way that I could do this was if it was the only choice—and that I had burned all other bridges. Because if I got a normal job, pretty soon, I would be caught up in that rhythm and would start to feel okay about my life—and I would feel that my dream would just gradually disappear. And I wanted to keep that hunger, keep that hunger burning. Because hunger was the only thing that I thought was my advantage."

Stallone said his wife didn't understand that at all. They had vicious fights. It was freezing; they had no money. One day he went to the New York City public library because it was warm. He didn't plan on actually reading anything, but he was hanging out there and sat down on a chair near where someone had left a book. It was the poems and stories of Edgar Alan Poe.

Stallone started reading it and totally got into it. How Poe had lived, how he died, what really happened, Stallone studied all of the details. Tony asked him, "Well, what did Poe do for you?" Stallone told Tony, "Poe got me out of myself. He got me to think about how I could touch other people—not worry about myself so much. And that made me want to become a writer."

Stallone began to write screenplays but nothing worked, and he and his wife were still broke. He didn't even have $50 to his name. But finally, he sold a script called *Paradise Alley*. Big success! He told Tony he sold it for $100 and that felt like a ton of money. Stallone was so thrilled and thought, "Yes, I am on my way."

Unfortunately, selling that script actually never led to anything (although he did produce *Paradise Alley* many years later). Stallone kept going and going and going and going. Finally, he was so broke he sold his wife's jewelry. He said, "Tony, there are some things in life you should never do . . . and that was basically the end of our relationship."

She hated his guts so much. Broke, they had no food, no money, and the one thing Stallone loved most in the world was his dog.

This is where the story gets really good. It is painful but a great illustration of why you should never quit.

Stallone was so broke he couldn't even feed his dog. It was the lowest day in his life. He stood outside a liquor store and he tried to sell his dog to strangers for $50. Finally, one guy negotiated with him to buy his dog—his best friend in the whole world—for $25.

Stallone walked away from there and just cried. Heart wrenching. But he still wouldn't quit.

Then providence set in. Two weeks later, he was watching a fight between Muhammad Ali and Chuck Wepner, who was getting bludgeoned but kept on coming back for more. He wouldn't give up. And Stallone had an idea. He started writing as soon as the fight ended, and he didn't stop. He didn't sleep. He wrote the entire movie script in twenty hours straight.

Right then and there. He saw the fight. Wrote the movie. Whole thing. Done. Stallone told Tony he was so excited that he was shaking. He really knew what he wanted. He knew why he wanted it. And he took massive action to get it.

But now that he had the script to *Rocky*, he still had to sell it to an agent. Some read it and said, "This is predictable, this is stupid, and this is sappy." Stallone said that he wrote down all the things they said and that he read them the night of the Oscars when they won. The greatest revenge can sometimes be massive success.

He kept going and trying to sell it and no one would buy it—and he was still broke.

But finally, he met two agents who read the script and believed in it. They loved it, and they offered Stallone $125,000 for it. Wait! What? Tony told Stallone: "My word, you must have been out of your mind."

Stallone definitely was. But he said to the agents, "Just one thing though, guys—you have a deal based on one thing. I gotta star in the movie." They were like, "What? What are you talking about? You're a writer!" Stallone pushed back, "No, I'm an actor." And they said, "No, no, no . . . you're a writer." He pushed back to them again, "No, I'm an actor. That is my story . . . and I'm Rocky. I gotta play Rocky. I gotta play the starring role."

They said, "Look, there's no way that we're going to pay you $125,000 and take some no-name actor and stick you in the movie and then throw our money away. We need a star. Take it or leave it." So, as Stallone left the room he said, "If that's what you believe, then you don't get my script."

Again, this is a man who was dirt broke, and $125,000 was more money than he had seen in his lifetime. Yet he walked away, because he knew his destiny and why he was committed to it.

The agents called Stallone a few weeks later, brought him back to their office, and offered him a quarter of a million dollars for his script, but he still couldn't star in his own movie. Stallone turned it down. The agents came back with their final offer of $325,000. They really wanted this script. But Stallone said, "Not without me in it." They said no.

They finally compromised, and they gave him $35,000—as well as a revenue share in the movie so that Stallone would share in the risk with them. The bottom line for the agents was that they didn't think the movie would work so they were not willing to spend a bunch of money on it.

They invested only $1 million to produce *Rocky*. It grossed $200 million.

But here's where it gets really interesting. Tony asked Stallone, "So what did you do? Even at $35,000, it's not a quarter million but it's still a lot of money when you don't have $25. What's the first thing you did?"

Tony figured Stallone went out and partied or something. But he didn't. He told Tony that he went to that liquor store where he had sold his dog and stood there for three straight days hoping the guy who bought his dog would come back. He wanted to buy back his dog.

On the third day the guy walked by. Stallone couldn't believe it. And there was his dog, too! Stallone looked at him and said, "Sir, you remember me?" It had been about a month and a half since he had sold him his dog.

The guy said, "Yeah, yeah, I remember."

Stallone said, "Look, I was so broke; I was so starved. He's my best friend; I'm sure you love him, too . . . but I gotta have him back, please; I will pay you $100 for the dog. I know you paid me $25; I will give you $100."

And the man said, "Absolutely not, no way. It's my dog now; you can't buy him back."

And Stallone said to Tony, "You know how you say, 'you gotta know your outcome'? Well, I knew mine, so I kept changing my approach. I offered him $500 for the dog."

The guy said absolutely no way. Stallone offered him $1,000 for the dog. The guy said, "No amount of money will ever get this dog for you."

Tony asked him, "So what did you do?" Stallone said, "I knew my outcome so I decided to take massive action. I just kept changing my approach until I got my dog."

Tony asked him, "So what did it cost you?" Stallone said, "$15,000 and a part in the movie *Rocky*!"

The dog in *Rocky*, "Butkus," was Stallone's real dog. That's the dog he bought back for $15,000.

If you're committed, there is always a way. You just have to keep changing your approach.

You were meant for greatness. You are instilled with an abundance of talent and gifts. Please don't let something so small as fear—or your circumstances—limit all you were meant to be.

As my mentor Don Yaeger says, "Greatness is available to all of us *if* you are willing to do the common things uncommonly well."

Don't ever quit!

SUCCESS STORIES FROM BUSINESS OWNERS

Each person's definition of success can and should be different. The word *success* is a difficult word for business owners to define. Sometimes having models or examples to consider—or insights from a mentor—can make all the difference in sorting out the outcomes that matter.

The business owners I interviewed for this section are using their podcasts to grow revenue, expand their platform, and build their nation of true fans. But what I found so compelling during these conversations was that while each had similar goals, they also had their own personalized strategies to get there. My hope for you is that their stories will help you gain clarity on your vital priorities and, most important, how you define what a successful podcast looks like for you.

John Livesay, host of *The Successful Pitch*

John is a funding strategist who helps CEOs craft compelling pitches that engage investors in a way that inspires them to join a start-up's team. He partners with Judy Robinett at *Crack the Funding Code*, which gets founders funded fast. He hosts *The Successful Pitch* with investors around the world. As I noted earlier, *Inc.* magazine calls John the "Pitch Whisperer."

■

Q1: Give us an overview of your podcast and the advice shared during a typical episode.

John: I was helping tech start-ups with their pitch and they kept telling me, "This is great. I definitely need help and what I also need are warm introductions to investors now that I have this great pitch." I kept saying, "I don't do that. I don't know any investors." Enough people kept saying it to me that I thought maybe I should follow my own advice, and that is if your customers and clients are telling you something that they want and are willing to pay for, then maybe you should figure out how to get it for them. My podcast was my way of building up my network of investors so I could introduce my clients.

But, before I even started, I had to overcome what I call the "Three Faces of Fear."

When I get afraid to do something outside of my comfort zone, I need to put a face on it; otherwise it's just so overwhelming and so fearful. For me, the first fear was the Fear of Rejection, where I would say to myself, "Well, what if I invite someone to be on my podcast and they say, 'No thanks,' or 'Let's hear several other episodes before I accept.' I've learned from being in sales for the majority of my career that the key to rejection is you just cannot take it personally. I take it one step further and tell my clients, "Never reject yourself."

The second fear I had to overcome was the Fear of Failure. When you're starting a podcast or a business or anything, the Fear of Failure will knock on your door and say, "What if you invest all this time and all this money and nobody downloads an episode? Won't that be humiliating? Won't that be a waste of time and money?" Luckily for me, one of my guests was Jay Samit, who wrote a book called *Disrupt You*. In it he writes, "Failure is just feedback. Keep going until you get a zombie idea so great it won't die."

Then the third fear is the Fear of the Unknown. The list of things I didn't know about starting a podcast was a mile long, including what microphone do I buy? How do I edit this thing? How do I promote it? What questions should I ask? I'd been a guest on many shows, but I'd never hosted one, and it's very different being on the other side of the mic. I found the number of technology things overwhelming, and I thought, "That could be the thing that stops me from doing it." Then, I found someone who does it for you. Collaboration is the secret to overcoming the Fear of the Unknown.

Q2: Why did you start your podcast and what are two or three of the biggest impacts it has had on your business?

John: It separates you from everybody else. When I used to go to events, and people would say, "Oh, what do you do?" I always said, "I help start-ups craft a pitch and make introductions to investors." Now, I say, "I host a podcast where I interview investors who share with me their criteria on what they look for when they hear a pitch. The response is now, "Oh. You're a journalist?" That was a big ah-ha for me. That part really changes how you position yourself.

The biggest impact was I got to meet the amazing and wonderful Judy Robinett as my second guest. Judy wrote a book called *How to Be a Power Connector* and has been doing venture capital funding and helping people for over twenty years. She started sending me people to help with the pitch . . . and they started getting great results. Then she said, "Why don't we go into business together and start *Crack the Funding Code*? You're all about the pitch and the storytelling and the selling and I'm all about strategic introductions and the financials."

Second, the guests that I've interviewed are amazing. Like Guy Spear, who along with another investor, paid over $600,000 at a charity auction to have lunch with Warren Buffett. And I interviewed him. I would never have gotten to talk to somebody like Guy if I didn't have a podcast. Guy said, "Well, how can I help you?" I said, "We're looking for start-ups who need help with their funding and help with their pitch." He said, "I started Entrepreneurs' Organization Israel, let me introduce you."

Third, I turned ten of my favorite episodes into a book called *The Successful Pitch: Conversations on Going from Invisible to Investible* because it really is eavesdropping in on those conversations with people that you would never be able to have a conversation with, but you get to eavesdrop in on the book from me interviewing them on the podcast.

Q3: What is the most critical skill for a business owner to master in order to be successful at podcasting?

John: I would say the most critical skills are empathy and listening. One of the investors told me on my podcast that the more empathy you show for your customer, the more you understand that customer and can solve that problem. The more you can put yourself in the shoes of your guests and respond to what they're saying, make them feel heard, and then summarize what you're hearing for the audience as the takeaways, that, in my opinion, is what it takes to be really great as a podcast host.

Q4: You've had some impressive success with your podcast. So, let's flip that. What do you consider to be your biggest obstacle or challenge to building momentum?

John: I would say the biggest challenge, after I got over the Three Faces of Fear and was actually starting to do it, was letting go of the need to be perfect. The irony is that I constantly coach my clients to let go of perfectionism and focus on progress, that is, be a "progression-ist" not a "perfectionist." When I took my own advice, I said, "I'm not going to be great the first few probably. I won't embarrass myself or make the guests feel uncomfortable, but I'm not probably going to hit it out of the park the first two or three." Just be gentle with yourself when you start anything new. Nobody starts off perfect.

Q5: What has been your most unexpected surprise during your podcasting journey so far?

John: That there would be a book and I would be on TV. I've never dreamed that dream. That was beyond anything I could've even imagined. I just wanted to do it to build my network of investors so people would hire me to help them with a pitch and make those introductions. I never dreamed I would meet my business partner, turn it into a book, or that I'd be going to Nashville, Tulsa, and Portland and doing TV here in Los Angeles all because of the podcast.

Q6: Do you have any final advice—anything else you want to share with business owners who may be considering starting their own podcast?

John: Just start—take action and don't do things that aren't in your sweet spot. Keep your intention on how can you can serve your listeners.

Vera Fischer, host of *System Execution*

Vera began her career in residential real estate, working her way up from leasing agent to property manager. She segued to operations manager for the first privately held cognitive rehabilitation clinic in Austin, Texas. In 1993, Vera launched her career at GSD&M, an internationally known advertising agency. After various positions within several Austin-area agencies, Vera went client-side to Forgent Networks. There she managed and implemented a multi-million-dollar marketing budget for several years. In 2004, Vera founded her agency, 97 Degrees West, in Austin.

■

Q1: Give us an overview of your podcast and the advice shared during a typical episode.

Vera: The podcast focuses on systems and processes for successful companies. Because of what I do in the marketing and branding world, I've met with hundreds of business owners. And the recurring theme in the discussions is that getting certain ideas or implementing a new product or implementing a new service is quite difficult from a process perspective, especially if they're not used to processes, or they get overwhelmed, or they're not into logistics.

I love processes, and I like systems, so one of my best gifts on my bucket list would be to go see the Amazon warehouse and how they actually get things packaged up. That's highly interesting to me. Also realizing that there wasn't a lot out there from a podcast perspective, so I said, "Hey, that's a great subject matter, and it's something that can keep going, and it's very personable because lots of people do it different ways. There's no one right way to do systems."

Q2: Why did you start your podcast and what are two or three of the biggest impacts it has had on your business?

Vera: I had been really doing a lot of research the past year before I actually launched it and really tried to understand how to get something like that off the ground. Through that research, I realized that podcasting is a new medium and I felt like there was an opportunity to be on the front end of it.

Also what is fascinating about it is that I have a very specific type of audience so it's this one tool I can use to have a deep connection with my audience and my guests. In the world of business, for most of us, unless of course you're Apple, you're not trying to reach the masses. You should be trying to reach a very specific type of audience that fits your criteria. It also gave me a voice as a business owner and as the brand of an individual. It allowed me to really research and explore what I like and also have an opinion about it.

The impact it's had on my business has been amazing. My network has exploded. I spend a good amount of my time following up with all of the opportunity. That's another key is that when you are starting something like this, you've got to be ready to follow up on every opportunity, every connection, and every introduction.

There is no way I could have met the people who I'm connecting with now and interviewing had I not started the podcast. Now I'm bringing value to these folks.

I get to be my own media channel because rather than walking up to the folks and saying, "Hey, this is what I do," I literally can say, "I'd love for you to be on my show." People get so excited about that. I have no plans to stop. I think it's just going to get better and better.

Q3: What do you think is the most critical skill for a business owner to master in order to be successful at podcasting?

Vera: You have to want to educate—especially from a business perspective. You're there to teach your listeners something: a skill, how to approach life, how to approach business, how to do something within their business, and if that doesn't come as an innate talent to you, or desire, it won't be fun. It's supposed to be fun. You should be energized by it.

Q4: You've had some impressive success with your podcast. So, let's flip that. What do you consider to be your biggest obstacle or challenge to building momentum?

Vera: It's hard to get guests at the beginning, and you should launch with at least ten podcasts in your queue. When you don't have a website or your podcast is brand new . . . you really have to find people willing to be interviewed without really knowing or seeing a lot of information about your podcast. But don't give up. Just keep going. In the beginning I literally, if there was a prominent business person I connected with, I wanted to interview them regardless of whether or not they were the right fit from an industry perspective. Just to help build some initial credibility.

Once I get them to sign up through my online scheduling link, and by the time that I get on Skype with them, they had already been communicated with several different times via email and text. We have a very professional Guest Advocacy System. By the time I get on Skype with them, they already know that it is a credible situation. I've never had anyone say, "I just don't think this is the right thing for me. I don't want to do the interview."

I solved this initial challenge in an interesting way. In my business, my role is sales, marketing, and finance. I spend a good part of my day understanding digital and really participating in that. I think that has made a huge difference. Through that, because I monitor our company's Twitter and my personal Twitter accounts, I started inviting people via Twitter, and shockingly they said yes. I couldn't believe it at first. Now it's even easier because I have a proven concept.

Q5: I know you track where you invest your time as well as your productivity— so how many hours do you typically invest each week toward your podcast? Where are you spending the time? What are your vital priorities as it relates to your show?

Vera: My guests are my vital priority. I probably spend two hours a week recruiting guests. It's getting easier because people know about my show. Whoever gets interviewed, I have a really great referral as well. Guests say to me, "Oh, I have a great person who would want to be on your show," and they'll send them to me. That part is getting easier, and I'm not spending as much time. As far as the interviews are concerned, they are usually anywhere from thirty minutes to sixty minutes and it depends on how many I have scheduled for the week, so it could be one hour or five hours out of my week.

The key is that I am not involved in the execution of all of this stuff. My role is to connect, have the interview, focus on that, and then my team takes care of everything else. I can't imagine if I had to do it on my own and do all of the editing, and the promoting, and everything like that. That would probably take up twenty hours a week. In my opinion, it's critical that you have a team that's managing and executing on all of that, where you're just focused on the good stuff—the interviewing and the guests.

Q6: What has been your most unexpected surprise during your podcasting journey so far?

Vera: That all of these incredibly intelligent people who have so many accolades and all of the cred, if you will, that goes with those people, they're just regular people. They're funny, and they deal with crazy schedules just like everybody else, and they've got kids, and they've got life things that are going on. They say to me, "What can I do for you? How can I help you?" Wow.

Q7: Do you have any final advice—anything else you want to share with business owners who may be considering starting their own podcast?

Vera: Podcasting is like taking a left turn. If you are taking a left turn and you see a car coming, you've got to commit. You can't stop in the middle of the road—you must follow through. Podcasting is definitely a commitment. *It's not a toe dip. You're either in or you're out.* Once you're ready to go—commit.

Drew McLellan, host of *Build a Better Agency*

Drew is the top dog at Agency Management Institute (AMI). He has also owned and operated his own agency over the past twenty years. All through the year, he straddles the fence of working in his own agency and working with 250+ small to midsize agencies in a variety of ways. He works with agency owners in peer network groups, he teaches workshops for owners and their teams, and he does consulting. His *Build a Better Agency* podcast reached number one in iTunes' New and Noteworthy shortly after launch.

■

Q1: Give us an overview of your podcast and the advice shared during a typical episode.

Drew: My podcast is an offshoot of my business, Agency Management Institute, and so as one might infer from the word *agency* being in both of those names, my audience is narrow. I serve agency owners and agency leaders in advertising, marketing, PR, media—those kinds of agencies that are what I call small to midsized. They might have one employee up to about three hundred employees. They are privately owned so the owners are still invested in the business, not only financially but it's where they spend their days.

My guests then are equally focused. When I sort of screen for who would make a good guest the question I ask myself is, "What could they teach an agency owner?" For me that gets easy because not only do I have that business, but I still own my own agency. I'm able to look at it from the lens of, "Can I learn something from these people in terms of running my agency?" That means my audience can as well. My guests have ranged. They're really a wide array of people in terms of their skill set, so everyone from CPAs who can talk about how to build your agency's value before you sell it, to an intellectual property attorney who talked about protecting trademarks, to people who own an agency, who've built an agency from scratch, or who've left a big agency to go out on their own.

So I really try to come at it in terms of who can help agencies be better, be more profitable, build a better entity, have better employee relationships. Anybody who can talk about any of those topics is game for me as a guest.

Q2: Why did you start your podcast and what are two or three of the biggest impacts it has had on your business?

Drew: I think like most things in business there are intended consequences and then there are surprises, so my intended consequence was to broaden AMI's digital footprint—to create a platform that was more interactive and allowed me to share with my audience expertise beyond my own expertise. I've owned my own agency for twenty-one years, and I've been doing this AMI gig for almost a decade, so it's not that I don't have a lot of knowledge around running a better agency, but there are certain things that guest Sharon Toerek knows because of her expertise as an IP attorney that I'm never going to be able to speak to with the same influence and authority she can.

I wanted to add even more value than I'm capable of doing on my own; hence, I need super-smart guests who have expertise outside of my own small sphere of knowledge. That's some of the unintended consequences, so I knew that I'd be exposed to more people. I knew that that would over time trickle into workshop registrations and other things, consulting gigs, all that sort of thing. A couple of things came out of it that I really hadn't expected.

Number one, the trickle of opportunity from podcast guests to workshop attendee has been greater and faster than I thought it would. So that's awesome.

It's not just workshops, it's consulting gigs, and AMI runs peer networks where agency owners come together and become like a Vistage group, but everybody is an agency owner. There have been more members joining. All of the things that AMI offers have benefited from the podcast, but some of the unintended or what I didn't really think about, or maybe went out of my primary goals are, I now have deeper connections with all of those guests, and that serves my audience in a couple ways. One, I have people I can connect agency owners to when they need a specific thing. I'm a much better referral source now to be able to connect them to these experts.

Number two, at a lot of the workshops and AMI peer networks and some of the other things we do, I need great speakers, so the podcast has been a way for me to audition, if you will, the speakers to see if they would be good as a guest.

Number three, it's opened up some really interesting partnerships between me and some guests. We've been able to collaborate on things together. Projects that serve a lot of them also serve the same audience. It's deepened my friendship with those folks, and it's got me a lot more invites into industry events, so that's been great.

There's not been a downside—there's been much more benefit than I ever expected.

I think the model you teach, which is the Trojan horse of sales, where you're inviting as guests to your show people you would like to do business with, I think that's brilliant. It's just not what I decided to do. As you know, I'm talking to other folks about it all the time and suggesting that they think about doing that and that they talk to you. Because I do think it's spot on.

I guess I would put it this way—I'm accidentally getting more business out of my podcast guests because of how and who they are. I think when you have great intention about who you invite on your show you can do it at an exponentially faster and better rate, but that wasn't my goal so it's not the way I built my podcast, but I certainly think it's a smart way to build a podcast.

Q3: What is the most critical skill for a business owner to master in order to be successful at podcasting?

Drew: I think it's a combination of skills, but I think the most important skill is that the host needs to be able to check their ego at the door. My job is to augment and put the spotlight on my guest and their expertise. I do that by listening really hard to what they say and running it through my filter of, "What else would an agency owner want to know about that?" I'm not talking over them. I'm not trying to jump in and show how much I know about it, but I am listening super hard. I am asking follow-up questions and trying to stay out of the guest's way so they have as much airtime as possible to share expertise.

I'm always listening like, "What should I be asking next? What did somebody want to hear more about that or how would they want to drill deeper into this?" I'm trying to ask those questions because I don't want somebody going, "I can't believe he didn't ask X!"

Q4: You've had some impressive success, like reaching number one in iTunes' New and Noteworthy during your launch. But, what do you consider to be your biggest obstacle or challenge to building momentum?

Drew: I'm sure I have the same doubts that everybody had. "What if I suck? What if nobody listens? What if no one wants to be a guest?" At first there was the, "How much work is it going to take?" For me it was really, I don't want to say a confidence issue, but it's a new venture, "What if I'm not good at it?" You're in essence doing it live, so what if I say something silly? How do I recover from that?

What I discovered is, that the minute I again checked my ego at the door, I realized that it wasn't about somebody listening to me, it was about me cultivating this great list of guests and serving the guests well, which serves my audience. So, I allow my guests to have the spotlight and I allow them to really share their expertise and I prep them properly so it's like, "Look, there is no selling; this is not about you getting clients, this is about you generously sharing your expertise. Here are the kind of questions I'm going to ask. If you're not comfortable answering those questions, don't come on the show." None of that was about me. It was about serving up the best content for the audience by putting the guests in the best possible light.

It wasn't really until I had fifteen or twenty episodes in the can that I really knew that this was something that was going to catch on and take off even though the numbers were already suggesting that that was the case. I needed that sort of, "Wow, all of my guests are consistently really good."

I had my own rhythm in terms of how I approached an interview, and then it was like, I can't possibly stop doing this because it's so awesome and successful and people love it, and it's serving my business so well, why in the world would I stop? The only advice I have is, you kind of push through it because it's good for your business, it's good for your customer or clients, and it's good for you as a person, too. I learned so much from my podcast guests. It just makes me a better professional. It makes me a better person, so there's nothing bad about it. You just have to get over yourself to get it done.

Q5: I know you track where you invest your time as well as your productivity— so how many hours do you typically invest each week toward your podcast? Where are you spending the time? What are your vital priorities as it relates to your show?

Drew: The time factor was really my biggest fear. "Will I have time for this?" I own and run three different companies. I am the primary caregiver for my mom, who is in late stages of dementia, and I have a twenty-three-year-old daughter, who, any of you who are a parent know, requires time and care and attention as well. My life is very scheduled. I am going at a full speed all the time. The idea of sitting and watching a television show without doing something else—I don't know what that's like.

I was very concerned about shoving something else into my calendar. So I will say this, and again in full disclosure, I quickly partnered with Predictive ROI to do the back end of my podcast. I'm a firm believer in recognizing where my own strengths and weaknesses are and doing what I do best where I can get the greatest return, whether that's in a personal relationship or that's money in a business or whatever it is, and recognizing that I cannot be all things to all people and so I need to pay for expertise that I don't have.

I had no desire to learn how to create a relationship with iTunes and do all the editing of the podcast and all of that so I turned to Predictive ROI and said, "I want you to produce my podcast for me. I will source the guests; I will interview the guests. I'll help with the Show Notes and things like that, but the whole technical side of it, I don't have the time nor do I have the expertise to do that really well."

The time investment on the front end was greater. We had to get all that stuff set up and even though I didn't do most of it, I had to sort of at least vote on some things. I was worried because of my schedule and, I guess, let's add to my, "Here is what my life looks like." I was on 188 planes in 2015, so I also travel a ton and I'm in a lot of all-day meetings, so I was really worried about having enough interviews so I didn't go dry one week. My podcast is a once-a-week podcast, so I wanted to have twenty or thirty interviews in the can before we went live, and I think I ended up with about twenty-five.

Obviously the time investment to do that was greater, but for me that's half a year's worth of podcasts. After the initial push, there are some weeks where I do little to nothing. I might approve the Show Notes that someone else has written for me. I might write a little intro that is going out on my blog or on Facebook when the show goes live, but there are some weeks that I don't do anything. For every podcast episode I would say I invest about thirty minutes to the guest, send the guest an email, which is a preset email that I just fill in a couple of blanks and sign them, inviting them to be a guest.

Then your team has everything automated so they go and find my schedule, they choose the time that works for them, they sign up for the interview. It gets out into my calendar so I know they've signed up, and then they're automatically sent the questions and reminders and all kinds of stuff that I don't have to think about at all. I will have about thirty minutes of prep to get the intro ready and to get my list of potential questions ready and all that sort of thing. Then I spend forty-five minutes or an hour or so doing the actual podcast interview.

I upload that into Dropbox and then I'm done. Then my team, which is your team, edits the podcasts; gets it ready; and submits it to Google, Stitcher, and iTunes; writes all the Show Notes; does all of the stuff in the background that I would never have time to do. Makes sure that the audio quality is great and coaches me on things that I can do better, all of those things.

With today's technology I have recorded podcasts in probably every state of the union. I have a really high-quality microphone, and it's very portable. I can take it with me and so (A) the podcast is fluid and flexible enough that it works around the rest of my life and (B) it's easy to do anywhere.

I will say this, if I can pull off a weekly podcast episode, anybody should be able to—not because I'm superhuman, but my life is just so calendared and scheduled that if I can figure out a way to fit it in, it really can't be that big of a burden.

I thought it would take more time than it did.

It flows nicely with the rest of my world, and now literally I'm at a conference or whatever and I'm saying to somebody, "Oh, you know what? You'd be a great podcast guest," and I am from my phone shooting them the template email, and boom they are signing up while we're standing there talking, and it's all so easy and seamless and the value proposition for me.

It's been so good for my business. I can't even imagine how good it's going to be for my business three and four years from now. So the time investment is really minuscule compared to the value. *I also can't even imagine how valuable it would be to me if I were interviewing prospects I wanted to have as clients.* The value would be even greater. It's just not my business model. Even in doing it my way, the value is exponential compared to the time investment.

Q6: What has been your most unexpected surprise during your podcasting journey so far?

Drew: People are reaching out to me now to be on the podcast. I have people asking if they would be good guests, which is awesome. I'm getting more opportunity to speak at conferences and other podcasts, so again, remembering that one of my goals was sort of to expand my digital footprint, and today in marketing anybody who is not thinking about how to really amp up their thought leadership and demonstrate their expertise is missing the boat. In terms of a thought-leadership tool or a marketing tactic, this has been spectacular. It's rippled a lot of other benefits for me in terms of exposure. *Fast Company*, *Inc.* magazine, and other places like that—I'm being invited on a regular basis to write for because of the podcast.

It's a rare marketing tactic that there is sort of no downside. There really has been no downside to this. It's exceeded my expectations in every way possible.

Q7: Do you have any final advice—anything else you want to share with business owners who may be considering starting their own podcast?

Drew: The hardest part is getting started, it's having the courage to start, to have enough faith in yourself that you can do this and do it well. Whether you're going to do the back end yourself or you're going to hire a company to do it, however that works out for you, you've got to have the courage to step into this because it is an amazing business tool.

I have not talked to any podcasters who've actually done it, and stuck with it, and don't get more value out of their podcast than they put time and effort in. So it's a very rare investment on any scale where you're guaranteed a greater return than what you invest. I believe that podcasting is one of those things that if you do it with the right intention and you do it with the right level of professionalism there is no way you're not going to get more from it than what you put into it.

It has exceeded every one of my expectations, and I can't imagine a business that wouldn't benefit from it. So if you're thinking about doing it, I'm telling you, you should.

Stacy Tuschl, host of *She's Building Her Empire*

Stacy is a speaker, business coach, and the owner of the Academy of Performing Arts in Wisconsin. She is the author of *Is Your Business Worth Saving?*, where she reveals proven strategies for pulling entrepreneurs out of a rut and launching them toward business success. She is also the host of the brilliant podcast *She's Building Her Empire*, which became the number one podcast in iTunes' New and Noteworthy just forty-eight hours after launch!

■

Q1: Give us an overview of your podcast and the advice shared during a typical episode.

Stacy: I do three podcasts a week: Monday, Wednesday, and Friday, and for two of them, Monday and Wednesday, I interview high-achieving entrepreneurs and then Friday is my solocast day. I love getting in front of these entrepreneurs, asking them, "Do you believe in work/life balance? Does it exist? Define that for me?" I love it because you get such different answers each and every week from everybody, and I think that is one of the best things that I'm doing is making sure that my answers aren't something that I'm going to get this typical cliché answer every time.

I love mixing it up, and giving my audience just something different every single time.

Q2: When you and I talked about platform building in Episode 174 of *Onward Nation*, you shared your three steps of collection, engagement, and conversion. Give us some more foundation. How do you define each of these steps and what are some of the ways they tie into the success of your podcast?

Stacy: Those three words sound so easy and everybody thinks they're doing it, but they're not doing it at the level they need to see that conversion they want. For me, the collection is the opt-in. You know, always having something of such value that people are surprised and just blown away that you're giving it away for free. That's for sure step number one.

Then, once you have that freebie out there, they're opting in; now you've really got to engage, and I think that's where people start to fall short. They don't have the funnel setup, they don't have the sequence actor, and one of my big things I do with my freemium, my freebie, is I've got a private Facebook community and now these are getting to be a little overwhelming for people.

Monday through Friday, I'm giving content so people say, "I've got to check it out today. I've got to see what she's putting out." That's such a great place to engage because they're there, they're commenting. I can comment back, so I make it part of my daily routine where I'm in Facebook Live, giving a free video training inside that group and then engaging with everybody that's commenting and sharing and liking. Then, once you have that setup and they're engaged, if you can do number one and number two really well, number three of selling and converting them is so simple because they're ready and willing because your free stuff is so great. They can't imagine what you're going to over-deliver on with the paid version.

Q3: Why did you start your podcast and what are two or three of the biggest impacts it has had on your business?

Stacy: I was already listening to podcasts and getting such amazing value out of the people I was listening to, so I immediately saw it as this amazing platform to give value to my community. That was really what made me think, "Okay, this could be something I could do." I wasn't positive if I would be good at it or if I would like it, but I just knew that I should try it and see where it goes. The biggest impact I'm going to tell you are the relationships that I'm building with my guests. It's unbelievable the people that I've interviewed on my show.

These are the people I've actually looked into some of them to consult with. I would have to pay $500 an hour to get on the phone with some of these people that I'm interviewing, and it's crazy that I get to, for free, pick their brain for thirty to forty-five minutes. It's just unbelievable, the content and the information that they're giving to me. It's like free mentorship with these incredible, high-achieving millionaires.

I think another thing, too, with this is the opportunities that are coming out of it, when they go, "Hey, would you like to be on my podcast?" So now they're on my show, they're starting to like me and go, "She could really give value to my audience, too," so I'm getting opportunities like that and then affiliate opportunities. People are emailing me and saying, "Hey, I loved your show. I love your audience. Would you mind doing this type of promotion coming up and be a partner with me and get an affiliate?"

It's just amazing what has come off of this. My foot is now in the door to getting into an hour with them over lunch or just something to work my way in that I don't know that I would have the opportunity if I didn't have that podcast.

And last week alone, I had two different people email and say, "Hey, I've got this going on. Are you interested in partnering?" These were just two occurrences that happened last week as a result of the podcast.

Q4: What is the most critical skill for a business owner to master in order to be successful at podcasting?

Stacy: I struggled in the beginning with how much do I say, how little do I say, what should you be giving out, and I think if you could practice interviewing somebody, it doesn't have to be on a podcast. Practice is crucial. I'm at episode number 90 right now, and I can just tell when I'm listening, when I'm going back and listening to certain podcasts, how comfortable I'm feeling talking with somebody and communicating and it's really just a conversation between two friends. If I could have understood that in the beginning, I would have realized how much I should be talking, should I give my point of view, or do I say, "Oh, very interesting. Next question." It was just that balance of how much I say, how much do I give, and you have to realize people are listening to your show.

Q5: You've had some impressive success like reaching number one in iTunes within forty-eight hours of your launch. But, what do you consider to be your biggest obstacle or challenge to building momentum?

Stacy: Understand that everything is a system, everything is strategy, and you just have to have the right people on your team, and the right guidance.

Hitting number one in iTunes wasn't something that just happened. That was a strategy. That was me really putting a system in place and pushing, and to hit number one, and to try to be on that top of the charts, it all comes down to four things and it's rating, reviews, subscribers, and downloads. You've got to create that list before you even launch. I made a list of all these different people that I could personally email, personally reach out to, and write emails that didn't feel like a mass email. It felt like I was one-on-one saying, "Hey, Stephen, is there any chance you could go and rate and review my show?"

There was just that conversation, too, to really sit back and go, "I know I need to hit X amount of people and I know I need to try to get that credibility of having ratings and reviews," because let me tell you, I've been trying to get on certain podcasts or have people on my show, and they'll say, "We don't get on a certain podcast until they have at least fifty ratings and reviews," and not in a way that they're better than me, but they're saying, "A lot of podcasters will start and they'll stop and this just shows that they're sticking around, they're serious about it, and this podcast is really going to get aired."

Q6: I know you track where you invest your time as well as your productivity—so how many hours do you typically invest each week toward your podcast? Where are you spending the time? What are your vital priorities as it relates to your show?

Stacy: I have been doing just once a week on Wednesdays. That's my podcast day and I batch them. I just find that when you're in the groove and you've got that set of interview questions, it's just so easy to flow from one interview to the next versus trying to do this actually one on Monday, one on Wednesday. Batching has been great. I typically interview three people a week to keep me staying on top of my calendar. Now, even though only two air a week, you'd be surprised how many people reschedule at the last minute, apologize, and say, "Hey, I'm so sorry. I can't do this today, but I'm on your calendar for next week."

Q7: What has been the most unexpected surprise during your podcasting journey so far?

Stacy: I think we all have that self-doubt of, "Am I going to be good enough? Do people want to listen to me? Will guests want to be on my show?" We don't give ourselves enough credit. I thought in the beginning, "Who am I going to get on the show when I don't have anything out there, there is no podcast, and I'm asking people to be interviewed on a podcast?" but I mean, even right out of the gate, I was able to get some amazing people in episodes 1 through 10. Don't sell yourselves short. People will look into you, they'll look into other things that you're doing, so they were checking out my live broadcast and my website, and my book, and that was giving me credibility.

Q8: Do you have any final advice—anything else you want to share with business owners who may be considering starting their own podcast?

Stacy: One of the big things people don't realize is that that first email invitation needs to look so professional and it needs to have everything in it. I get so many of these emails now because people are asking me to be on their show. I can't believe sometimes that I have to email back and say, "Well, who is your audience? What questions? What can I bring? I need to know what I can bring to your audience, because I don't want to waste your time and I don't want to waste my time either."

I jam-pack my invite email with everything. I get so many people who don't respond to the email—they just immediately book with me.

Lori Jones, host of *Integrate & Ignite*

President and CEO of Avocet Communications, Lori brings top retail, consumer product, business-to-business, and nonprofit organization knowledge and experience in all aspects of integrated marketing to clients. Her experience with Fortune 500 brands and entrepreneurial start-ups enables her to contribute a keen understanding of the intricacies of today's businesses. Lori is also the host of the brilliant podcast *Integrate and Ignite*.

■

Q1: Give us an overview of your podcast and the advice shared during a typical episode.

Lori: I explore the nature of what it means to be an entrepreneur. Every episode is crafted to make people think, and spark some of those aha moments, or just to illustrate how important a truly integrated business and marketing strategy is, and really provide a solid blueprint for people to lead to success and longevity. At the end of the day, our guests are a mix of start-up entrepreneurs, and Fortune 500 CEOs from different industries. If our listeners seek out the advice, inspiration, or gain a good laugh, or just one of those kicks in the pants that they might need, then I feel that we're pushing out good content.

We explore several different topics through each interview. We talk about philosophy, and leadership, and what qualities it takes to succeed in today's fast-changing business climate. We then get into approach. What is their approach to leadership? How do they integrate their internal departments, and, more important, which is the premise behind the podcast, what are they doing from an integrative marketing standpoint? What has worked? What hasn't? What can they share with our listeners? We then move into the third segment of the interview, which deals with obstacles. We've all had a lot of obstacles in our business lives, in our personal lives—and challenging times that could have devastated us. We glean insight from these CEOs and business leaders on what they did to overcome those obstacles. We end the podcast with success and defining what success means to them as an individual, as an organization, and talk through some of the processes that they deploy on a day-to-day basis for big wins.

I love it. I get so excited when I get to record a podcast, talk with a CEO, or a business leader, or a start-up entrepreneur about what is in their head. I'm constantly learning, which is important to the mindset I have with all of our team members as well.

Q2: What does a "personal brand" mean to you and how can a business owner use that to create differentiation?

Lori: Personal branding is about making a full-time commitment to the journey of defining yourself, as a leader, and how it shapes the manner in which you serve others. It should represent your value, and consistently deliver to those whom you serve, or those whom you report to, or those, ultimately, whom you want to be able to impact positively. The most important thing about personal branding is that it's not about self-promotion.

People don't care about all the accolades, and all the awards, or anything like that. You don't showcase yourself. You showcase your passion. Managing your personal brand requires that you be a great role model, that you be a mentor, that you've got a voice, that people can learn, grow, and depend on.

Q3: Why did you start your podcast and what are two or three of the biggest impacts it has had on your business?

Lori: I'm very inquisitive, and I love to learn. I always want to know more. From a business standpoint there have been several benefits from my podcast. Here are a few: It's all about building top of mind awareness, or "TOMA," surrounding integrative marketing approaches for small and big businesses. My podcast has enhanced our agency's position as a leader in our space. You cannot dream up the quality of content we are now producing from our episodes. The content was a major reason I knew going into this that the podcast would benefit our business.

The other point I want to make is we're able to open up doors that probably would not have been opened without the podcast. In our industry, there are Fortune 500 companies that get contacted consistently—and constantly—from marketing firms like mine. This has allowed me an entrée that is unique and different, it establishes credibility out of the shoot, and it builds context for the prospect. All of that would be very difficult to do otherwise.

Q4: What is the most critical skill for a business owner to master in order to be successful at podcasting?

Lori: I have a script going into every podcast, but I have to be able to think on my feet and ask questions throughout the interview that are poignant and relevant based on a response that has been given by my guest. I listened to many, many podcasts, and this is something that you do very well—you pivot.

I've got my script going into each interview, and I plan to ask similar questions in each episode, but 50 percent of the content generated is typically based on questions that have been asked while I am pivoting in response to what a guest shared.

Q5: You've had some impressive success with your podcast. So, let's flip that. What do you consider to be your biggest obstacle or challenge to building momentum?

Lori: I don't believe most people are fully aware of the strength of podcasting. They might even be a little afraid of it. They might even ask themselves, "What is a podcast?" Despite the explanation that I provide guests up front, some prospective guests are afraid about the amount of prep time they might need. So our podcast has become a good litmus test. If people we talk to, if there's a great brand out there that ultimately we want to become a part of, and they don't understand what a podcast is, that's a good litmus test for us to know. Maybe they're not quite up to this sort of solution. That has been a big epiphany since we started the podcast.

Also, guests are very busy. Case in point, we found out two and a half weeks ago that one of our clients was going to appear on ABC's *Shark Tank*. We had two weeks to finalize the plans and get ready for the show. I ended up having to cancel a couple of podcasts that week, which I felt horrible about, because we were stretched in getting ready for a viewing party with 250 people, all of the media relations, and press that were coming through my office that week. I felt horrible for having to cancel, which was one of my mantras going into this is—that I would never do that. But the point is also this: Your guests will end up rescheduling, and canceling, some of them two and three times, because of the same reasons. They get so busy that they end up having to reschedule things. Don't take it personally. It's going to happen and just stay on top of it.

So back to our client and *Shark Tank* for just a minute . . .

It was one of the most amazing things I've ever been through in my business career. I mean, how often does that happen? That one of your clients ends up on *Shark Tank*! So we used our podcast to help introduce it.

We did an encore interview with our client. We did a pre-show interview. We knew that the *Shark Tank* episode was going to air on October 7th—so the week before ABC aired the episode we aired our podcast based on four simple questions ABC would allow us to ask and talk about.

That helped to raise awareness about how our client was going to have their appearance on the 7th. The press leading up to it won interview after interview. It was a total blast. After the show aired, the following morning, we did another interview, post-*Tank*, and talked through what we knew, what we could talk through at that time, regarding the fact that they had won, and that they had been funded. I asked what it was like being in front of the audience that night. What are you going to do going forward? All these great nuggets of content shared by our client.

We recorded that podcast the Saturday after the show, and we released it Monday morning. We also released a newsletter a week later. We wrote a story about what you need to consider when you are going on a show like *Shark Tank*. What you need to be aware of. What you can say. What you can't say. It was just an incredibly exciting opportunity for my agency. We had a blast, but what I'm also going to let you know is, off of this podcast, we got a call from another company that is going to be airing on *Shark Tank*, and we're going to be promoting their show as well, which all happened because of the podcast. Now, it's not just one—we're on number two!

And lastly, on the night of the event, we created an experience. Our entire marketing team was there, and we were live-streaming Google Analytics and social media data to the audience. They could see these huge spikes as the show was airing from coast to coast. We delivered an integrated plan, but we also created experiential components the night of the event.

Q6: I know you track where you invest your time as well as your productivity— so how many hours do you typically invest each week toward your podcast? Where are you spending the time? What are your vital priorities as it relates to your show?

Lori: I personally invest around ten hours a week with interviews, reviewing content, and prospecting additional guests I'd like to have on the show. My vital priorities include getting the big brands, and the big leaders on the show, which can really take months to accomplish. Our team invests about fifteen hours a week creating the content, newsletter, Show Notes, and the actual podcast episodes from a production standpoint. All in, it's about twenty-five hours a week for our entire team.

Q7: Do you have any final advice—anything else you want to share with business owners who may be considering starting their own podcast?

Lori: We all, for the most part, have these incredible personable brands out there, but they're on paper. They're words. They're visual. They might have a voice, but there's nothing better than the *actual* voice. Your actual voice delivering content! To me, a person's voice adds that personal connection to their brand, and to their content—and that is very valuable to the personal brand.

Kelly Hatfield, host of *Absolute Advantage*

Kelly is a cofounder of Enginuity Advantage. She has been in the recruiting and HR field for twenty years and loves serving others. Kelly and her business partner have built three successful companies with the purpose of helping others succeed and delivering remarkable results. Kelly and her team strategically align themselves as the "Partner of Choice" with clients and strive to be the first place to call when clients are looking for extraordinary service, quality, and reliability. Kelly is also the host of the outstanding podcast *Absolute Advantage*.

■

Q1: Give us an overview of your podcast and the advice shared during a typical episode.

Kelly: The *Absolute Advantage* podcast is for entrepreneurs, leaders, achievers, and emerging leaders. Our goal of it is to shorten our audience's path to success. We're gathering insights and learning from the world's most successful entrepreneurs, leaders, and achievers at the top of their game. One of the reasons I started the podcast was because I realized that as entrepreneurs or leaders, it can be a lonely place or you're questioning yourself a lot: "Gosh, am I doing the right thing?"

I think hearing from other leaders and entrepreneurs—their stories, their concepts, their insights—with the goal being if every person can take away one pearl of wisdom each episode that they can apply and improve their business, improve their leadership skills, then it was a win. We talk a lot about leadership, cultivating people, building teams, personal development. These topics are all relevant to who our audience is.

But there is something else. In our business, we own a couple of recruiting firms, so we've gained a unique perspective from being entrepreneurs, building our teams, scaling, and doing those things. And we also meet with thousands of companies who are our clients and we hear their pain and we hear what they're going through or we may be having conversations and can identify some of their pain before they even realize what it is.

That perspective and background uncovered some common themes, which are leadership, cultivating people, building teams, and building culture. A lot of our discussions—because, again, our business as recruiting is about attracting talent and retaining talent—so our podcast serves two things, which is as an entrepreneur and feeling like that circle shrinks a little bit the more successful you get, so these discussions have become a bit of a system of support and encouragement.

And then there was the aspect of, "Gosh, all of these people, including ourselves, are going through a similar kind of pain, or the same kind of situations or issues keep arising." I wanted to help solve for that. Through our podcast, we are building a community around that.

Q2: Why did you start your podcast and what are two or three of the biggest impacts it has had on your business?

Kelly: I have spent over twenty years in the recruiting business and really was looking for something and seeking something that would allow me to make more of an impact on people than I already was—to be able to reach more people and have a greater impact.

The second thing was to build a community where people weren't feeling like they were alone, where we were covering a lot of topics that many people were going through.

Then I thought, "Okay, well, how can we do this? How can I accomplish this and bring more value to our clients as well?" That's really where the whole idea of doing the podcast spawned with the goal of creating more impact and wanting to bring more value to our clients.

The feedback I'm getting in terms of the topics, people reaching back out and saying, "Hey, I just listened today to your duo cast about hiring slow and firing fast. Some of that information that you shared, can we talk a little bit more about it?" They're really starting to look to us even more so than they ever did. Some are clients we have worked with for a long time while others are clients who are fairly new where they're looking to us as the experts in our field. The podcast is positioning us as subject matter experts.

Q3: What is the most critical skill for a business owner to master in order to be successful at podcasting?

Kelly: I would have to say active listening, being engaged and present in the conversation with your guest, hearing what they say, reflecting it back to them and/or highlighting some key points they shared and making sure you have clarity about what it is they're saying for your audience and to help your guest shine.

Having been a guest on podcasts myself, there have been times where I felt like, "Okay, I'm in the right place. This host is hearing what I have to say. They're trying to get the best out of me for the audience. What I'm saying matters. They're getting it." Helping a guest feel comfortable is a way to go a little bit deeper with the conversation; maybe your guest will then share another example, another kind of pearl, or another layer of information. The great podcast hosts are the ones who really pull the best out of their guests, which means they engage at another level.

Q4: You've had some impressive success with your podcast. So, let's flip that. What do you consider to be your biggest obstacle or challenge to building momentum?

Kelly: That darn impostor syndrome! For me, it was overcoming something in myself that was saying, "Okay, what is it that you've got to bring to the table?" I'm interviewing these amazing people and at the same time thinking, "Okay, why are they going to want to talk to me?"

On the flip side, too, one of the things that I didn't realize is that 90 percent of the people who are guests on the show are thinking the very same thing. I've reached out to some amazing business owners in my network; it's been a challenge getting them to be a guest because they're having the very same thoughts, like, "Oh, yeah. Well, I've built this great business but I'm not sure what I am going to have to bring to the conversation." And I have said right back to them, "Well, that's exactly why I want you to be my guest, because you've built this amazing business and started out of your garage, and it's this multi-million-dollar business now with hundreds of employees."

Checking ego at the door is huge. I have a business coach and we were having a conversation about the show. It was like getting a glass of cold water thrown in my face when he said, "When did this become about you?" I said, "You know what? You're right," and he said, "Where's the Kelly who is always about bringing value to people and about this being about the audience and key points that need to be made with the audience and in giving of yourself and giving to the audience? When did this become about you and how you feel?"

It's all about the audience and the guests. This isn't about me in any way.

Q5: I know you track where you invest your time as well as your productivity—so how many hours do you typically invest each week toward your podcast? Where are you spending the time? What are your vital priorities as it relates to your show?

Kelly: Five to six hours a week for our two episodes. My vital priorities are prepping for the shows and the recording time. Because we're partnering with a team like Predictive ROI, once I'm done recording the interview, all I'm doing then is uploading that recording into an Airing Schedule, and then my production team takes it from there. I don't have to do all of the other things associated with the podcast.

That was one of the things that was really important to me, too, as, first of all, I didn't have the time to learn about everything there is to learn about podcasting. There are professionals out there who can do all of these, and I would have paid double, triple, quadruple the amount had I tried to do it on my own, screwed it up, and then had somebody come and fix it for me. It's a fantastic production, and I've got a great team who supports me.

Q6: What has been your most unexpected surprise during your podcasting journey so far?

Kelly: We've had some amazing guests on the show who are masters at building an awesome culture within a company. Applying some of those lessons and seeing the results internally with our team as a result of implementing the thoughts and ideas from our guests has been awesome.

Q7: Do you have any final advice—anything else you want to share with business owners who may be considering starting their own podcast?

Kelly: Don't let fear get in your way. If this is something that you are seriously considering, and are excited about, don't let fear get in the way. Push yourself outside your comfort zone. There have only been upsides to doing this podcast for me. I can't think of one negative thing. It's only brought positive things to my life and to my business. Just because you want to do a podcast doesn't mean that you need to know everything, all of the technical aspects, and all of the marketing components. There are people out there like Predictive ROI who can help you with that. I haven't seen any downside. Just do it.

David Mammano, host of *Avanti Entrepreneur*

David has started seven businesses from scratch, was named to *Inc.* magazine's list of the 5,000 fastest-growing companies in America, is host of the *Avanti Entrepreneur* podcast, and is a TEDx speaker, author, and adjunct professor at the University of Rochester.

■

Q1: Give us an overview of your podcast and the advice shared during a typical episode.

David: I started the podcast because I kind of wanted to have a forum, a conversation, for "the rest of us." I love reading *Inc.* magazine, *SUCCESS Magazine*, *Forbes*, and *Fortune*, etc. Often you'll see on the covers these massive superstars, the founder of Uber, or the founder of Go Daddy. I mean all great entrepreneurs, don't get me wrong—I want to be them tomorrow; there's no doubt. But the fact is I'm reading these articles and I'm thinking, "That's just not me right now." I'm not going to go out and get $100 million of venture capital. I think most people reading these articles are probably a lot like me. They've created businesses from scratch, maybe bought a franchise, maybe took over a business, but at the end of the day, we're not the sophisticated venture capital dudes in Silicon Valley.

We're main-street entrepreneurs who roll up our sleeves and work our freaking tails off, and our investment money that we get from the outside is from making sales. The certain realities are, we're out on the streets, we're making it happen, we're getting our MBAs in the streets. I wanted a podcast for "the rest of us," meaning, let's share some really good practical advice and experiences from people like me or a few steps ahead of me.

Q2: Why did you start your podcast and what are two or three of the biggest impacts it has had on your business?

David: I'm a lifelong learner. My podcast really is, at the end of the day, a very selfish way for me to learn. I'm getting guests on whom I really love and respect, and kind of want to suck their brain for knowledge, so I just get to ask them tons of things that I'm wondering about their success. Taking notes as I'm talking to them, asking questions, and listening—so I'm learning.

Second, my podcast is really good for my business. One of my main businesses is the Avanti Entrepreneur Group, where I help business owners either grow their business or I help people start their business. I have a whole strategic process on taking businesses to the next level. I'm a coach for business owners. It turns out that I get a lot of people asking how they can start working with me, so my podcast has been good for attracting prospects and customers.

Q3: What is the most critical skill for a business owner to master in order to be successful at podcasting?

David: I think what I've learned so far is just becoming a really good interviewer. Really paying attention, being curious about the path, the way the conversation is going, and asking good questions because what you get out of guests is amazing. The first few podcasts I felt like I was talking too much because that's what I do, but now that I've kind of learned a little bit, what makes a better podcast in my opinion is when I'm actually doing very little talking. So I would say become a really good questioner.

I've taken Dale Carnegie courses, and one of their top things that they teach is: The way to get people interested in you is to become interested in them. People love to talk about themselves and their successes and share experiences. People end up liking you more as a person, and respect you more, if you ask them really good questions and allow them to talk and share their experiences. It just makes a person feel good when they're able to talk about themselves and even their failures, if it's a learning lesson, because they'll feel good about helping others.

Q4: You've had some impressive success with your podcast. So, let's flip that. What do you consider to be your biggest obstacle or challenge to building momentum?

David: Well, I'm 100 percent a salesperson. I love people, and it's my superpower. I should probably be selling 99 percent. But, when it comes to technology, and the process that goes along with the behind-the-scenes tech, I'm terrible. I get anxiety about it. I can picture myself breaking out in hives. I know what I do best. I sell, I coach, and

I love content. I love to write, and do videos, so I should be spending most of my time doing that, like the podcast. Developing relationships with guests and asking questions during the interviews.

So working with [the] Predictive ROI team—I did not have to do any of the stuff that I'm not good at, which was such a joy. I probably would not have launched a podcast on my own because of all the production and technology involved.

Q5: I know you track where you invest your time as well as your productivity—so how many hours do you typically invest each week toward your podcast? Where are you spending the time? What are your vital priorities as it relates to your show?

David: I'm spending probably two hours—three hours at the most—per week on my podcast. There's about forty-five minutes to an hour of doing the podcast. Then I would say there's another hour or so when it comes to finding guests for the show, then sending them some prep material so that we're good to go.

Q6: What has been your most unexpected surprise during your podcasting journey so far?

David: How much I freaking love it! In fact, Diana on my team, she has said, "I think you found your calling." When I ask people what I'm really good at, I often hear that I'm a connector, a host, and this is kind of the perfect role for somebody like that. I feel like if I could become the Jimmy Fallon of entrepreneurial podcasting, then I'll be a happy man. I don't have to be the star—I can be the host. It feels natural to me. I want to do more.

I also didn't expect how good it would be for my business. It's a really nice piece of what we're doing here. Now, I don't think somebody should get into podcasting just with the sole purpose of increasing business because you probably won't be focusing on good quality content, and I think that you have to have very good quality content from the heart so people want to listen to you.

Q7: Do you have any final advice—anything else you want to share with business owners who may be considering starting their own podcast?

David: There's no reason why you shouldn't give it a shot. At the very least you're going to learn a ton from the people you're interviewing.

Just do it. You'll get energy from it, you'll build your network, you'll build your reputation, and you'll build your credibility as a business owner.

Mitch Stephen, host of *Real Estate Investor Summit*

A nationally known real estate entrepreneur, trainer, and consultant, Mitch has purchased more than 1,300 houses in his hometown of San Antonio, Texas. He is also the author of two books, *My Life & 1,000 Houses: Failing Forward to Financial Freedom* and *My Life & 1,000 Houses: 200+ Ways to Find Bargain Properties*. Mitch is a high school graduate who never stopped learning from books, seminars, and webinars and is a fine example of what "on-the-job-training" can produce in a person. Mitch now teaches others how to become financially independent and invest for more than just the typical lump-sum check.

■

Q1: Give us an overview of your podcast and the advice shared during a typical episode.

Mitch: I was just trying to find a place for the people in my niche, which is flipping houses or creating cash flow, so they can become financially independent. I wanted to have a place they could go to—I wanted to reach the world as much as I just wanted to reach my niche. We are attracting people who I think we can help—people who are looking to be financially free.

I started the podcast because I know just like with my Tuesday night coaching call (I held a call every Tuesday night for the last six or seven years), it has made me a smarter person as well as delivered value to attendees. It's like the teacher gets the benefit: I might bring ninety-nine pieces to the puzzle; because I've been in the business a long time, I've got a lot of pieces of the puzzle already figured out. But every now and then, someone raises their hand in the room and gives me an extra piece that I didn't know existed. Then I'm thinking, "Oh my gosh, this changes everything." Or, "How in the world did you figure that out?" Or, "Where are you finding this list of people?" Then I think, "I have to start doing that!"

If you think the guys who are listening to me are getting smart, I'm getting really smart by listening to everybody. And the podcast helps me in the same way.

Q2: Why did you start your podcast and what are two or three of the biggest impacts it has had on your business?

Mitch: I was trying to get more people into my mentoring program. I was trying to move from thirty to forty people a year to fifty or sixty to seventy people a year, just to see if I could. If you do all this stuff just for the money, it becomes kind of a drudgery or it's an obligation. I just recognize in my life that activity begets activity. The more active you are and the more things you're trying or doing, just the more people you bump into, and the more possibilities and the more options come to you.

I thought, "Well, I haven't done this before, I wonder what this would bring me?" And I have no idea exactly what it'll bring me. I knew my goals were to get my sales up and to get some more followers, but what kind of followers am I going to find? What kind of opportunity will they have in store for me? I don't know, but it's fun to go out there and try it and see what happens.

Then the other thing about it is, if you ask a really successful CPA to go to lunch so you can rake his brain, get some tax advantages from him, he'll say no. If you tell him you want to interview him, he'll run to your door. It's the same conversation, but one is I'm stealing from him and the other one is I'm honoring him. If you want to talk to them as an interview, they'll talk to you for two hours. If you want to rake their brain, they're not going to talk to you—they want your money.

Q3: What is the most critical skill for a business owner to master in order to be successful at podcasting?

Mitch: You have to listen. Listening is the hardest thing I'll ever do because I like to talk. Listening is hard for me. I recommend slowing down. To let my guests take the conversation where they want to go and for me to shut up and let them finish. That's my personal challenge. I'm kind of ADD; some people would call me high strung, or tightly wound.

Q4: You've had some impressive success with your podcast. So, let's flip that. What do you consider to be your biggest obstacle or challenge to building momentum?

Mitch: My biggest challenge is that I would like to interview some more famous people. We often think of them as unattainable because we are not a TV station or some other media channel. I decided this year I was going to make this a goal. As a matter of fact, I just got off the phone trying to contact Doug Flutie because I wanted to have a conversation with him about underdogs. I talk to a lot of people who are underdogs. I love a good comeback, and you know who was the king of comebacks in the NFL? Doug Flutie! He was small for the giants he was playing around.

Someone said, "Well, how in the world is his story going to relate to real estate?" I said, "Well, his story's a little broader; it's not about real estate, it's about overcoming the odds, incredible odds." How did he do that?

Q5: I know you track where you invest your time as well as your productivity— so how many hours do you typically invest each week toward your podcast? Where are you spending the time? What are your vital priorities as it relates to your show?

Mitch: The setup was the hardest part. After the initial setup it's three to five hours per week because we air three episodes per week, and I invest about one-and-a-half hours per episode.

I don't have to do a lot of rehearsal or scripting because I live the subject that I'm talking about with our guests. And my guests live the subject, too, so they don't need a script either.

Usually what we do is we map out the initial four questions, just so we get off to a smooth start. I also spend a little bit of time reading their bio, how I'm going to introduce them, and then we're off.

Q6: Do you have any final advice—anything else you want to share with business owners who may be considering starting their own podcast?

Mitch: Yeah, don't do it by yourself. Don't think you have to do it all. There are experts out there—find them to help you.

The reason I never did it sooner is because I thought I had to do everything myself. Now that I have a team in place—and for only three hours a week of my time to have three episodes go out per week, that's an incredible reach. That's not too much to ask—three hours a week to be available to the world and to build this body of work and content. When I complete the first year, it will be 150 interviews. What are the chances that I hold 150 interviews and something good doesn't happen? I think the odds are in my favor. Something is going to happen!

Lee Caraher, host of *Focus Is Your Friend*

Lee started Double Forte in 2002 as a new kind of communications firm designed to provide the best service in the business. Previously executive vice president at Weber Shandwick, president and founder of Red Whistle Communications, and vice president of SEGA, Lee has managed multiple offices and hundreds of people of all ages and was named in the "40 under 40" by *PRWeek* magazine.

Q1: Give us an overview of your podcast and the advice shared during a typical episode.

Lee: The purpose is really to help marketing people who are just bombarded with, you know, tactic, after tactic, after tactic. Do this, do this, do this, and do this, right? No company, and I've talked to companies who now are $10 billion companies or $100 million companies or haven't-made-revenue-yet companies, and no one has enough money. No one has enough time. No one has enough people. There's always more to do, no matter what size the company is, more to do than you can do. The purpose of the show is to focus on what matters so you can actually get traction.

My guests are chief marketing officers, chief revenue officers, chief communication officers, or CEOs. It sort of depends on the size of the company. Those people who are responsible for connecting a company with its audience and causing them to act. Sometimes at Google it's a director. If you get a director at Google, that's an "intergalactic president of something else" at another company. It just really depends on the size of the company, but the responsibility is to communicate and engage an audience that moves that audience to act.

My favorite question I ask everybody is, "If you had a hundred dollars and you had two activities and the two tasks, the two programs, cost $70 each, what would you do?" Frankly, I have a point of view, which is clear in the title of the podcast, *Focus Is Your Friend*, that you should do one thing. However, no one is really paying attention to that when I talk to them. I've gotten every answer from do one thing and save the $30, take the $70 and add $30 to it to do that one thing, do both, negotiate. I mean everyone!

It's really interesting to see the wide range of answers on that very simple question that I thought I would get the same answer. There's a rationale for everything!

Q2: Why did you start your podcast and what are two or three of the biggest impacts it has had on your business?

Lee: There are two reasons I had to start my podcast. One is to provide a place where my employees can tap into the wisdom and insights that I'm bringing. It's important they get to hear me—the bigger we get and the farther away we are. Right now I'm in New York, and we have an office in Boston, and we have an office in San Francisco. My podcast allows me to be present on topics important to our business.

Then the second purpose was I get asked a lot by people, "Lee, can I pick your brain? Can I pick your brain?" I'm like, "You know, I got no more brain to pick, frankly." This podcast allows me to do that as well.

Then third, what's been so far with the people I've interviewed, they're all people I know. I mean I've been around the business for a long time. I'm that old. I've worked at really large companies that have really large clients so I've had a lot of contacts. I don't have an excuse to talk to them all the time. This has been a great excuse to talk to those people and to (A) find out what they're doing, and (B) almost half the time I have an idea for these companies after I talk with these people. We may not be the ones who implement it, but that person on the other side I'm interviewing has always said, "Thank you, that's a great idea." Then sometimes it comes back, "Could you guys do that for us?" Sometimes we can, sometimes we can't. When you are in the service business, which most of us are, being helpful is the key to staying on top of mind.

Q3: What is the most critical skill for a business owner to master in order to be successful at podcasting?

Lee: I think it's the same skill you need to be a good leader, which is listening, and not listening to respond, but listening to hear. This has been the hardest thing for me—to not talk over my guests. All I want to do is, "Oh, yes, great idea." My early interviews are not as good as my later ones. I'm always listening for the nugget. Then trying not to talk over the person when I find it.

Then when you're doing that, listening between the lines, it sounds like you're taking that in, resisting the temptation to talk over or to jump enthusiastically into the conversation. Then you reflect back what you took out of that piece as the nugget.

And at the end of the show I'm summing it up by saying, "Here are the three things I'm taking away from this. You have something totally different, but what I'm taking from this show is bum, bum, bum." I try to be reflective that way. When that process is followed—from the beginning of the interview to the end—rapport is growing.

Q4: You've had some impressive success with your podcast. So, let's flip that. What do you consider to be your biggest obstacle or challenge to building momentum?

Lee: Time is challenging. Then making sure I don't ask too much of our guests before they show up. I've been a guest on over 450 podcasts. Some of them want pre-calls, and "Can you fill out this big form with all this stuff." As a podcast guest, I'm already giving you an hour of my time. I try to keep being a guest on my show simple.

Then sort of getting over the fear of asking people to be on the podcast. Like, "They're not going to want to be on my podcast." You know what? Sure, why wouldn't they? They like talking to me.

Q5: I know you track where you invest your time as well as your productivity–so how many hours do you typically invest each week toward your podcast? Where are you spending the time? What are your vital priorities as it relates to your show?

Lee: What I do is probably three to five hours a week. Three to five hours a week recording because I always want to be a little bit ahead. I record the interview and then as much as I can I record the Friday episode right after the interview so it's fresh in my mind. It's forty-five minutes of recording.

Then once a week I'm looking at where I am in the cycle and who hasn't said "yes" yet and adding people to that. Probably three to five hours of recording in my little studio looking at the questions, getting ready, preparing, understanding who's coming, who's my guest, what do I need to know about them, and then actually recording the two shows. Then fifteen to twenty minutes to approve the Show Notes and the promotional tweets for each show and probably another hour to just make sure that I'm on track with everything. Like, do I have the right guests? What am I missing? Do we have to mix it up a little bit?

It's a lot of time. It's not insignificant.

Q6: What has been your most unexpected surprise during your podcasting journey so far?

Lee: Some people really come prepared. They really take it seriously. I did all the thinking beforehand, right? I did a lot of thinking before I even wanted to do this. It took a lot of time to think about it. But my guests are really taking it seriously and some of them are nervous. People are nervous about talking on podcasts, which is really ironic. Impostor syndrome–lack of confidence abounds.

NOTES

Introduction

1. https://youtu.be/ABCNDZIdKa0.
2. https://www.sba.gov/content/small-business-trends-impact.
3. http://www.waspbarcode.com/small-business-report.
4. https://www.sba.gov/content/small-business-trends-impact.

Chapter 3

1. Hill, Napoleon. (1937). *Think & Grow Rich*. New York: The Ralston Press.

Chapter 5

1. http://contentmarketinginstitute.com/2011/11/content-marketing-inbound-marketing/.

Chapter 6

1. http://kk.org/thetechnium/1000-true-fans/.

INDEX